FLEX-PERTS

Getting the best from flex in a world that's ever changing

GILLIAN
BR∞KES

Flexperts
First published 2023
Published by Gillian Brookes
www.gillianbrookes.co.nz
Copyright © Gillian Brookes, 2023

ISBN (Paperback) 978-0-473-67776-3

A catalogue record for this book is available from the National
Library of New Zealand

International edition printed and distributed by Lulu Press, Inc.

To Mum

Contents

"So, is flex the 'new normal'? Is our work here done? Well, no, it's not."

Annie Auerbach, *Flex*

Introduction

A friend of mine is a fantastic people leader. She's a communications specialist with a background in journalism. Let's call her Mia.

Mia leads a team of internal communications professionals for a relatively large organisation. She's the kind of manager who people choose to follow. When she's ready to move on and find her next role, people queue up to join her on the next part of her career journey. A technically capable communications specialist, empathic people leader, with a strategic mind, she connects the purpose of her work out to other people. Her team is highly motivated and delivers great results. She really is great at her job. Yet, even she finds managing a flexible team challenging. I'm writing this book for Mia.

You're probably quite similar. You're well practised and successful as a people leader and you love that part of your role. Well, you love it at least some of the time! I'm also writing this book for you.

We dive further into the definition of flex in Chapter 1, but for now let's define it as giving people choices about the hours, days and/or place of work.

The world of flex, and people's expectations about work, are dramatically different to how they were a few years ago. Managing a team in this context is hard work. You've got old tools in a new world and they just don't stand up to the job.

The Flex-Team Toolkit resources in this book are designed to help you navigate your way through those expectations. They will enable you to give people more of what they need to be at their best, while also delivering great-quality work, all as part of a positive culture across your team.

This is a highly practical guidebook. I step you through the Flex-Team Toolkit and bring it to life through several real-life case studies. There are pictures, diagrams and white space so you can take your own notes and scribble down ideas as you go. The book doesn't aim to persuade you that flexible work is a good or a bad thing – it's for the pragmatic, capable people leader who simply wants flex to work better than it does at the moment.

Visit www.flexteamtoolkit.com for a downloadable version of the Flex-Team Toolkit to give you everything you need when you're working with your team. You'll find tools, templates, tips and questions to guide you through this ever-changing world of work. When you get to a section in the book that has a relevant download, you'll see this logo:

Think of the Flex-Team Toolkit like a pick 'n' mix. You can choose the pieces you want, depending on what your challenge is and where you and your team are in your search for new ideas and support. There's more in the toolkit than you'll need at any one time. It's a menu to choose from, depending on your appetite. You don't have to eat it all at once. In fact, trying everything at once would be a bit overwhelming, and that's not what you need. Instead, read through the book and pick out the parts that resonate with you, based on what you and your team need most. Prioritise those parts of the Flex-Team Toolkit and pick up the downloadable templates to get you moving. You'll find that's the best way to accelerate your journey to becoming a flexpert.

Once you've read the book, you'll dip back into it as a reference guide. There will be more in here to help you and your team get more from what flex has to offer. Higher levels of productivity, retention and wellbeing are all on offer when we get it right.

Why I wrote this book

I became a flexible work specialist back in June 2019, following a 15-year career in human resources in both the UK and New Zealand. I've always seen the human resources profession as having potential to create better lives for people, as well as much better businesses. Before I dive into that, let me take you back a bit further.

Economics and its discontents

I have a geeky interest in wellbeing economics and how organisations can evolve to participate in a wellbeing economy.

I studied economics as my undergraduate degree. I loved it, and also realised towards the end of my studies that it was a well-modelled, persuasive work of fiction. The first time I came to understand this was in my final year, when I read *Globalisation and its Discontents*, by Joseph Stiglitz (2002). He opened my eyes like never before, helping me see the harm that economic policy can do to other countries and its role as a modern form of ideological control and imperialism.

People, their lives and their cultures were not considered in the economic models I had learnt about at university. We were all assumed to be 'homogenous rational actors'. "Really?" I thought. It seems to me that we do not all behave in homogenous ways; we all have our unique stories, hopes, dreams, fears and motivations. How do you create an economy with space for people as they really are, to bring out their best, their unique value and contribution? An economy that serves the best of us, individually and collectively. Not the other way around; the worst of an economy that demands that we mould ourselves to a uniform standard version of humans in service of generating monetary and economic value.

After university, I rejected the idea of going into banking or some other career typical of graduates from the School of Economics. I found myself drawn into human resources and leadership. To my mind it blended people with business and economics, and gave me some creative licence to explore ways of bringing out the best in both.

Alongside my career I continued to study, formally and informally. I kept geeking out on new economic thinkers, until I discovered wellbeing economics. These were my people!

People like Amartya Sen, Kate Raworth, Katherine Trebeck and Katrine Marcal have all inspired me to keep digging into this idea. From my interpretation of their work, I've been able to experiment with the idea that organisations can be productive and positive contributors to the wellbeing of people and the planet. It's not an inevitable burden that we have to live with, tolerate or compensate for. What if work and organisations could have a net positive impact?

Flexible work: my instrument of choice

Given my professional background in human resources, one way for me to play a part was to focus on flexible work. I'm interested in giving people more access to work – high-quality, meaningful work. I want to find ways for people to contribute their skills and experience to our organisations while also upholding the other important aspects of their lives.

When people are at their best, they are also able to do their best work. One important enabler for people to be at their best is to provide more autonomy, more choices. As Amartya Sen's work in wellbeing economics concludes, choice is critical for people's wellbeing. More choices about where, when and how work gets done creates more opportunity for wellbeing.

Throughout my human resources career, I could see that flexible work was moving forward, but at a slower pace than I was comfortable with. From 2012, when my eldest daughter was born, my personal experience was the challenge of caring for small children alongside my career, and feeling guilty almost all of the time. I was either not fully present when I needed to be with my kids, or never quite giving enough to my ever-demanding job.

I pushed the boundaries of what was considered 'normal' flexible work practice, which I felt compelled to do for so many reasons. As a leader in human resources I felt I could use that position to demonstrate what was possible and role model to others that combining work and family life was absolutely possible. I also wanted to create space for others to move into the new flex territory we were opening up and create the conditions for more flex practices and ideas to come to life.

Working parents have been an important cohort for me in my work for a long time. In August 2016, I created My Kids Village, a website designed to help working parents find local childcare. I also run an online Working Parents Network. I host regular online events to help working parents explore our unique joys and challenges as we work with a system of school and work that were never designed to coexist. Working parents are often the ones who continue to push the boundaries of how we manage work and home at this time-poor crunch point in our lives. They are the trailblazers showing us what's possible and it enables everyone else to follow.

This trend of flex being made available to those with caring responsibilities was visible in many countries' flexible work legislation, and at the time of writing, in some countries, still is. We will look at some of the legal considerations of flexible work in Chapter 1.

Annie Auerbach talked about 'parents as trailblazers' as an idea when she published her book Flex, and I've always really liked that frame.

Back to why I took up the flex specialist path. Pre-2019, although I was role-modelling flexible work, that act alone wasn't going to be enough to make an impact on, or accelerate, flex at scale.

I saw that no-one in my profession had the time, or headspace, to do the deep work required to redesign our approach to flexible work and change the pace at which it was adopted. In-house human resources teams, like those I was leading, were too busy with the daily operational demands of the business. We weren't able to provide the new tools and resources that could make the difference. When I decided to become a specialist I wanted to be the person to use my human resources expertise, my experience as a people leader and motivation as an amateur wellbeing economics geek, to do just that.

I was less than a year into my work as a flex specialist when the Covid pandemic came along. This created conditions for every business to pay attention to flex that we haven't seen before or since on such a global scale. So much changed in such a short space of time, and our collective focus shifted to remote and hybrid working.

This guide is my attempt to make that part of your job easier, and for you to get more of the benefits of productivity and wellbeing through flexible work. I want to make you feel safe enough to be bold.

Is this book for everyone?

Yes, this book is for every people leader because, ultimately, flex is for everyone in some form or another. Depending on the nature of the work you and your team are responsible for, you'll find some parts of the Flex-Team Toolkit more useful than others. For example, if your team is primarily face-to-face, such as retail, the remote work tools will be less relevant. However, your team will be well placed to explore flexible hours and days of work instead.

Case study

I was running a series of 'Flex Work' workshops for a large organisation. People from the facilities team were choosing not to sign up to attend. I had a chat with one of them when I arrived to set up the room.

"I don't think I'll come to the workshop. I don't get to work flexibly because I'm part of the facilities team. Everyone else can work flexibly, but we can't. We have to cover reception and sort out any problems that come up in the office. It's just part of the job."

"I'd still love you to come," I said. "Working from home is only one aspect of flexible work. If remote working isn't possible in your role then you can get creative with the hours and days of work instead. Is that something you and your team could look at?"

"I suppose so. I sometimes like to go to a yoga class at lunchtime but it doesn't always work out. Is it stuff like that we can think about?"

"Yep, that's exactly the kind of thing you can look at."

"OK," she said. "I'll see if I can come. I assumed it wouldn't be relevant."

After the workshop...

"Thanks for persuading me to come. I really thought this wouldn't be any use for me. I'd got stuck only thinking about working from home as flexible work, because that's all anyone is talking about."

Limits of the book

This book explores how to manage a team through varying the hours, day and/or place of work.

Flexible work requires the ability to flex. If there isn't any flexibility to begin with for you and your team, this book and its tools won't change that situation. The Flex-Team Toolkit will take your team's flexible work practice from good to great. It won't take a fixed work environment and convert it to a flexible one.

There are teams that operate with very legitimate fixed constraints. You might have a rostered team that has to deliver in person, for example, in healthcare. In these situations it can feel difficult to identify opportunities for flexibility. If that sounds like you and your team, you're not alone.

The Flex-Team Toolkit might feel like it's too much, too soon. Before you try out the tools here, you might first want to explore what could change and over what time period in order to give people more choices.

That might include:

- **Job design** to reshape the team's roles, creating more flex opportunities in a reshaped job
- **Technology** to change the way work can be delivered
- **Roster upgrade** to give people the ability to work the hours or days that they prefer.

Once your team has identified ways to create some flexibility and choices, the tools in this book will become really valuable.

Another limitation of this book is that it is not a comprehensive guide to managing every possible type of flex. For example, managing a job-share partnership or shortening the work week is not specifically covered.

Andrew Barnes has written a fantastic book all about shortening the work week, so if that's your focus I recommend reading *The 4 Day Week* (2020). Another great read is *Shorter* by Alex Soojung-Kim Pang (2020).

I haven't yet found a really comprehensive guide to job sharing, but maybe that will follow this one.

This book doesn't consider variables other than the hours, days or place of work. Flexibility of the work itself is an emerging frontier of flexible work, often referred to as job design or 'job crafting'. Job crafting is how you adapt and flex the design of the work itself. It considers what work you do, and how you use your strengths to create a role that maximises your contribution and value. It's not about when and where work gets done. Job crafting is a really exciting idea and one that I am sure we will all hear more about in the future. Some of the tools in this book could be adapted to support some forms of job crafting, but that is not our focus. If this is something you want to explore further, I recommend the work of Amy Wrzesniewski, Professor of Management at Yale University.

The tools, templates and resources in this book have been tried and tested by hundreds of people. Over 90 per cent of them agree that they have had a positive impact for their team and organisation. I hope you will too.

Part 1

Flex is complex

"If we invented work tomorrow, is this how we would choose to organize it?"

Gemma Dale, *Flexible Working*

Chapter 1

What is flex?

Before we get into the story about why flex is complex and what's driving it, I want to put some definitions around the meaning of flexible work in this book.

Not all forms of flex work in every context, but some form of flex is theoretically possible in any line of work. Flex is so much more than the ability to work from home. In fact, for a large proportion of our workforce, in-person work will continue to dominate. Let's explore how the workforce is shifting, at the time of writing, to three main categories.

Workforce distribution cake

Nick Bloom is a Professor of Economics at Stanford University and has specialised in studying remote work for over 20 years. He talks about the workforce in three tiers.1 I think of it like a cake.

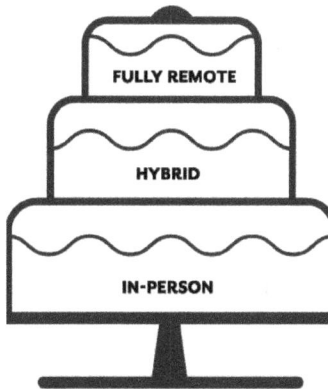

Layer 1: In-person

The first and largest tier is still in-person. This makes up about 50–55 per cent of the workforce in most developed economies, such as the US and the UK. These are jobs in industries such as retail, manufacturing and healthcare. If we only think about flexible work in terms of working from home, then we severely limit who it is for. We exclude people from flexible work opportunities before we have even started. That would be horribly ironic when so many leaders view flex as a way to build a more inclusive workplace.

Not all of the tools in this book will be applicable to you, but most of them will be. If you and your team are part of the in-person workforce, as you read this book, think about how you can use it to get creative with the hours and days of work. As you read the portions that explore remote and hybrid work, you might begin to consider whether there's a small proportion of the work your team does that could be carried out remotely. How could you create some feasible options for people to flex their place of work?

Layer 2 : Hybrid

The next and middle-sized tier is the proportion of the workforce who will be working in a hybrid way, at around 30–40 per cent. Hybrid working is a mix of working in-person and from home. It feels a bit like it's taking over, but it's not. It is growing, however. It's the brand new jargon for a way of working that has been around for a long time, but the adoption has accelerated at such a pace that it feels like uncharted territory. It's adding complexity to our teams and workplaces that we're not used to managing.

All the tools and resources in this book will be useful for you and your team. They are designed to help you safely explore new forms of flex and enable the current ones to function at their best.

Layer 3: Fully remote

This is the smallest tier of the workforce, at around 10–15 per cent. There is a small but growing number of fully remote workers. However, it is unlikely to become our new default any time soon. Bloom points out that remote work lends itself best to the type of work that requires skilled tasks that follow a process, where collaboration is less critical to the day-to-day success of the role.

If you have an entirely remote team, or people in your team who are fully remote, all the tools in this book will help you and your team get the best from your flex choices.

Defining flex

Flexible work means different things to different people. To put some consistency and boundaries around it, I think in terms of giving people choices about the hours, days and place of work. Using these three variables there are infinite ways in which people can flex. As I mentioned in the introduction, I'm yet to find a job that can't offer some flexibility for at least one of these variables. If people in your team want to explore more of these variables, you'll find the 'Delivery' tools in Chapter 5 really useful, to give people the boundaries within which to try something new.

The menu I outline here is not an exhaustive list of flexible work options. It is a useful reference point for some commonly used types of flex that might help you and your team explore what's possible now and what isn't yet. The options aren't mutually exclusive. You can think of this as a tapas menu, rather than main meals. There is room for you to have more than one at any given time. For example, you might work part-time, in a hybrid way, using flexi-hours. Or work compressed hours remotely.

Flex menu

Flexi-hours

Working daily or weekly hours in a flexible way, such as flexing start and finish times, or taking a longer lunch break. May include core hours in the middle of the day.

Part-time

Regularly working a fixed portion and fewer hours than the standard full-time working week.

Compressed hours

Working agreed weekly hours in fewer days, such as full-time hours over four days or a nine-day fortnight.

Job share

One full-time role delivered in a shared way by two part-time people.

Remote working

Working from home or from somewhere other than the office/workplace some or all of the time.

Hybrid working

A working week that has a mixture of remote working alongside working from the office/workplace.

Flexi-leave

Buying additional annual leave to be used to reduce working hours or days. May be used to arrange an agreement for term-time working.

Shorter work week

Shorten the working week for the whole workforce with no reduction in pay, in exchange for higher productivity, e.g. the 4 day week.

Formal and informal

Flexible work arrangements can be formal or informal. The formal arrangements are when a change is made to a person's terms and conditions of employment.

If someone wants to reduce their hours and move from full-time to part-time work, for example, this needs to be formalised. This change impacts on their pay and that needs to be agreed by both parties, the employer and employee, and the changes then flow into the payroll system.

Alternatively, someone may want to work one day per week from home for the next three months to see if that helps them make progress on a project as well as reduce their stress levels. This could be handled easily through an informal arrangement, with no permanent change to terms and conditions.

An informal arrangement doesn't mean that nothing is written down. If someone wants to try out a new way of working, it's important to agree up front what that looks like in practice and any relevant measures of success. This is covered in more detail in Chapter 7, as part of the flex-team cycle.

Your organisation's flex policy

In your organisation you probably have your own policy and guidance around flexible work. It's important that you take that into account alongside the Flex-Team Toolkit. If you notice the ideas and templates in this book go against something in your organisation's policy, then it's best to talk these ideas through with your manager or the human resources team. Your senior leadership team might want to adopt them across the organisation in a planned way, perhaps with your team as a pilot.

If you go ahead and do something completely different to what's in the policy at the moment, you could accidentally create more problems than you solve, at least in the short term. Many organisations have rules, not tools, especially if they are at the 'Frozen' or 'Fragile' stages of flex maturity that we explore further in Chapter 2.

You could find the Flex-Team Toolkit drives you and your team towards forms of flex that currently sit outside the 'flex rules' in your organisation. I'm all for the 'seek forgiveness, not permission' approach to leadership, but sometimes it's best to bring others along with you on the journey.

If you're not sure, it's best to check with your peers, senior leaders and human resources team before you go ahead with the new Flex-Team Toolkit.

Legal framework

Depending on where you live and work in the world, you'll need to be familiar with the legislation governing how you treat formal flexible work arrangements. The law differs from country to country and some places have very little governing it at all. There is a lot of attention on flexible work at the time of writing, so it's worth keeping an eye on how that legislation might evolve in the coming months and years. It's unlikely to remain entirely unchanged.

Chapter summary

- Flex is defined as giving people choices in their hours, days and/or place of work.
- The flex menu is tapas style, not mains, designed to enjoy more than one form of flex at a time.
- The menu of flexible work options can stimulate thinking for you and your team.
- Check out your organisation's flex policy before you start using the Flex-Team Toolkit.
- Consider the legal framework around flex in the place where you live and work.

Chapter 1 notes

1. www.barrons.com/articles/ive-been-studying-work-from-home-for-years-heres-whats-coming-5164 1330825

"Who doesn't want to have the freedom to choose where to work and when to work?"

Heejung Chung, *The Flexibility Paradox*

Chapter 2

Why flex is fragile

Pre-Covid: flex was emerging

Pre-pandemic, there were plenty of organisations ready and willing to get more flexible about when and where work was done.

I live in Wellington, New Zealand. It's known as the 'coolest little capital in the world' and it's a great place to live and work. It's also increasingly expensive to buy or rent property. It was becoming fairly common for people to want to move further out of town, such as further north up on the Kapiti Coast or 'over the hill' in the beautiful wine-growing region of the Wairarapa. That trend was already driving more people to request working from home for a few days per week, and more employers were willing to give it a try.

New Zealand is also well known for its earthquakes. Just after midnight on 14 November 2016 there was a magnitude 7.8 quake in Kaikoura, near the top of the South Island. The impact here in Wellington, about 250km to the north, was huge. Some offices were destroyed overnight. Fortunately, because of the time of the quake, no-one was seriously hurt, but it was a massive wake-up call for how we got work done from that point on. Lots of organisations realised the importance of having the technology to enable people to work from anywhere. When you lose your office space overnight, your business continuity plan gets a big workout. Some businesses fared well while others were nowhere near ready to respond. After that I noticed many organisations invested in mobile technology and practised new ways of work that enabled people to work from anywhere at any time.

Wellington is not unique. Everywhere around the world, for so many reasons, we are waking up to the importance of enabling people to have more flexibility in where and when work gets done.

The pandemic accelerated flex

"The current demand for flexible working is outstripping the supply of available flexible jobs." –Gemma Dale, Flexible Work

When the pandemic hit, the shock had an overnight impact on how we work. Many countries went into lockdown at very short notice. Households all over the world were now the places where everything got done: school, work, family time and hobbies. We adapted to it with mixed success.[1]

The tough side of remote working during the pandemic was no longer having boundaries between work and home. The burnout that started to occur as so many of us tried to maintain pre-pandemic standards in all aspects of life began to take its toll. During lockdowns, people were reflecting that these standards couldn't be maintained.

This prompted the international discussion that began in 2021 about The Great Resignation, or The Great Reflection, as it was also referred to. 'The Great Resignation' was first coined by Anthony Klotz, Professor of Organisational Behaviour at University College London. He predicted that the pandemic experience would lead to many people rethinking their relationship with work and we would see pent-up resignations hit as the pandemic lockdowns eased. En masse, we were looking for new and different ways of earning a living while making space for the other important aspects of our lives.

Gartner Research in 2022 highlighted how the pandemic experience had in fact led many people to deep reflection and showed how this was playing out in our shifting attitudes to life and work.2 In their study they found that 65 per cent of people agreed that: The pandemic has made me rethink the place that work has in my life. (Gartner Survey)

Another well-researched problem that I've also found in my own work is that people feel disconnected from their colleagues. I discuss this further in Chapter 3.

This double-edged sword of benefits and challenges through

enforced remote work throughout the pandemic shows that there is a lot of potential value from it. It also shows we need to treat it with caution and be aware of its downfalls.

As we saw in the introduction, around 30–40 per cent of our workforce is now hybrid. As hybrid work becomes commonplace, it's critical that we all learn to do it better. With hybrid now a more standard way of working, many leaders I work with are finding it to be a mixed bag. There are some productivity benefits but also many disruptions.

No longer can you step into an office and gauge how people are doing. You can no longer read the mood of the room, because it's often an empty space, or a computer screen with mixed levels of engagement and visibility from participants. This relative explosion of hybrid working is a key driver of the fragility of flexible work, which we go on to discuss next.

Flex is shifting

When a change occurs at such a rapid pace, such as our recent experi-ence of a mass movement towards a hybrid way of working, there is a natural response to want to 'go back to normal'. It's a bit like the tension you get when an elastic band is stretched. The pull to resolve the ten-sion by going back to its previous state is intense. The brain's craving for certainty is a strong force, and many of us want to recreate the comfort of what was stable in our pre-pandemic world.

There is also a curiosity in many of us, as we've seen in 'The Great Reflection' research, about what else might be possible or available to us in the future. We don't all want to go back to what we used to have.

In terms of flexibility, here is a way I see these tensions and curiosi-ties playing out inside our organisations. They translate into four stages of flex maturity.

Flex maturity

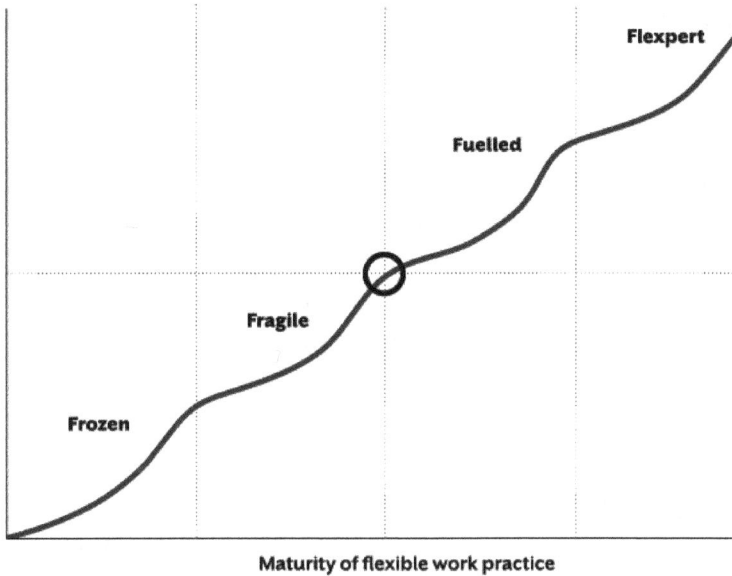

Maturity of flexible work practice

The graph above illustrates the four key stages of flexible work maturity that I observe in my work. There is a point of inflection, as organisations move from 'Fragile' to 'Fuelled', that this book is designed to get you through. Before we explore what it takes to make that shift, let me describe the four stages:

1. **Frozen**
2. **Fragile**
3. **Fuelled**
4. **Flexpert**

As you read through them, consider which one most closely describes your team and organisation.

Stage 1
Frozen: The ice sheet

Organisational culture

Flexible work requests are only considered when made formally. They are mostly granted to people with caring responsibilities. Most people work a default of full-time hours, Monday to Friday, and being visible in-person is highly valued. Some experience the culture as low trust and high control and don't feel comfortable asking for flexibility. There is a high level of consistency and certainty about where, when, and how work gets done.

Typical manager approach to flex

Managers feel very uncomfortable when they receive a flexible work request. Their default is to avoid flexible work arrangements. They don't want to create unnecessary complexity or to be seen as leading a team of people who are less committed than others.

What is valued most?

Presenteeism and management control.

Stage 2
Fragile: The melting ice

Organisational culture

Flexi-hours, part-time and hybrid work are considered normal. There is high value placed on the short-term delivery of tasks but when people are no longer in the office together as a default, connections between colleagues can become very loose. No-one is sure how far flex will go and what is considered acceptable. Rules are in place across the organisation to try and reduce the sense of chaos and complexity around flexible work arrangements.

Typical manager approach to flex

Managers feel uncomfortable as more people want to work from home or try other types of flex. Managers are increasingly stressed from having too many expectations from people in their teams and not enough structure to manage the growing complexity of arrangements. They often plug the delivery gaps themselves in order to make flex work for everyone in the team. Managers are cautiously allowing more levels of flex but rely on rules to limit the complexity. They don't want to be the team accused by their peers of taking it too far.

What is valued most?

Short-term delivery of tasks and management accountability.

Stage 3
Fuelled: Moving towards solid ground

Organisational culture

The impact of flex is regularly measured and team members are more accountable for delivering the work than they used to be because they highly value the autonomy they have been given. Some bolder types of flex are still yet to be tried but nothing feels off the table permanently because the benefits of flexible work are clear and visible to everyone.

Typical manager approach to flex

Managers are clear about why flex matters. They have reliable flex-tools that they regularly use with their teams. This has built their confidence to the extent that they are safe to experiment with new forms of flex. They have let go of the rules they used to rely on because they know that their flex-tools get better results.

What is valued most?

Experimentation, autonomy and team member accountability.

Stage 4

Flexpert: On new and solid ground

Organisational culture

The organisation has a great reputation for its flexibility and people value belonging to a place that enables them to do their best work while also having space for all other important aspects of their lives.

Typical manager approach to flex

Managers and teams have fluency with the tools that enable them to work flexibly as well as deliver high-quality work every day.

What is valued most?

Wellbeing, productivity and creativity.

Flex is fragile

At the time of writing, I see that most organisations are in the fragile state. No longer are we frozen in our approach, standing on what used to feel like solid ground. The frozen ice has begun to melt, and the ground is shifting and making us feel less stable and certain.

We couldn't have made it through the past few years if we'd allowed next-to-no opportunity for people to work in a more flexible way. But if that's where your workplace used to be, as we move to a post-pandemic context, there will be some who feel a strong pull back towards what was familiar and comfortable.

Furthermore, most organisations aren't yet clear about what the new solid land looks like, or even where it is. We are far from a new, comfortable space where we can work flexibly, knowing that it provides so many more benefits compared with our old ways of working. Benefits to both the employer and employee, a win-win, are still emerging and inconsistent.

To tip from fragile to fuelled, that critical inflection point, requires clarity of knowing where the solid land is and fuelling ourselves to get there. What we need is new practice with new tools and common language to make sure everyone knows what a win-win is and what it looks like in their context. We don't yet have those tools to help make sure that work gets delivered well, colleagues stay well connected to each other and people benefit from having more flexibility in their lives. Instead, we use an outdated practice with no clear structure. This leaves you as the manager feeling uncertain, trying to make the best of a difficult, complex situation, and getting on with it to make it work.

Fuelling flex

To get beyond this fragile state we need to create more certainty and clarity. We need to be clear about why flex is worthwhile and here to stay, as well as how it will be supported.

Creating that clarity requires **three key ingredients:**

1. Connection to **strategy**
   Where are we going?

2. Flex **leadership** style
   Who will get us there?

3. Reliable **tools** and practice
   How will we get there?

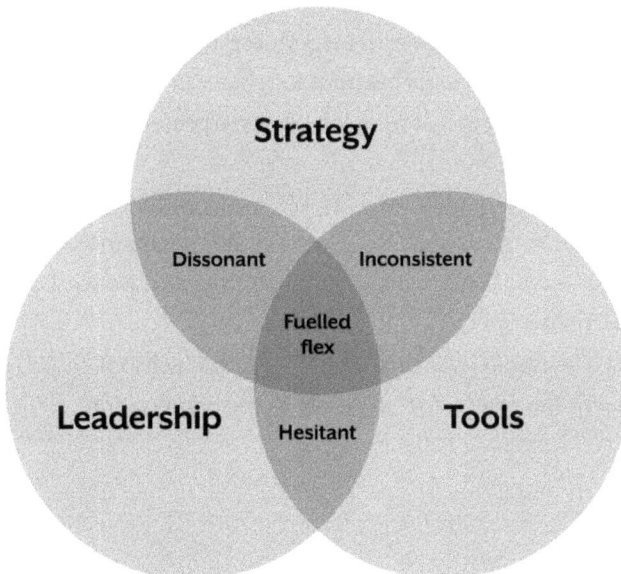

Key ingredient 1
Connection to **strategy**

The connection to strategy is a critical piece of the puzzle. So many people I work with find they can't trust that flexible work is truly supported in their workplace, and so they feel reluctant to make the most of it in case they're seen as work shy or pushing the boundaries of flex too far.

If you can make it clear why flexibility is important to you and the organisation's goals, then people will trust it. There are so many potential connections between strategy and flex. Here are some common ones that might fit for your team and organisation:

- Attract the right people to deliver on your organisation's growth strategy.
- Enable more diverse talent to grow their career within your organisation so that better-quality decisions are made at the leadership level.
- Retain a hard-to-recruit workforce in a tight labour market.
- Reduce the risk of burnout for your workforce by offering ways of working to suit people's personal preferences.

When you can articulate why flexible work matters, you're then able to get into the detail of what a win-win actually means in your organisation and your team. That's where high trust lives and we will come back to this in Chapter 3.

As a leader in your organisation, people will look to you to understand why flex matters strategically to the organisation.

Questions to consider

- Are you clear about why flex matters to your team and organisation?

- How consistent is flex's connection to strategy between you and other leaders?

- What assumptions do you have about who flex is for, or how it should be used, that could undermine the strategic purpose of flex?

When you're clear and consistent you give confidence to your team that flex is here to stay. You can do that by talking about why it matters, the benefits you experience for yourself personally, as well as across the team and more widely for the organisation.

Measuring flex

In terms of backing up the strategic importance of flex, people know that what gets measured gets done. If flexible work and its impact is never measured people will know that it doesn't really matter to you. Not in a serious way. Here's how I think about the measures for flexible work. Like any good measurement tool, it needs triangulation to be robust, so here's a triangle!

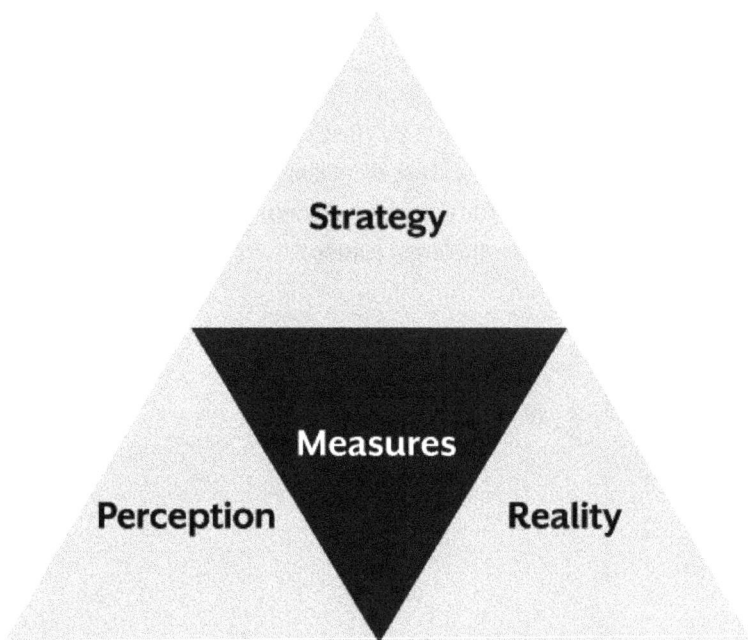

Strategy: Flex and its strategic intent

First, is flex contributing to the strategic intent as everyone hoped it would?

For example, if you wanted to achieve a higher retention level for hard-to-fill roles, how is retention going? Are people staying in their roles for longer than before? How is that going over time? You can also look out for unintended consequences, such as gender bias in hiring and promotion opportunities. For example, a powerful question to test yourself with is, "If more women are working flexibly and taking up the opportunity on offer, is this having an impact on their career progression and how they're perceived in the workplace?" The next step is to also track meaningful measures that will let you know of unintended consequences.

Reality: Flex and its uptake

Consider monitoring the uptake of the flexible work options on offer in your organisation.

Many of my clients feel great when they find that over 70 per cent of their people are working flexibly. When we dive into that a bit further, it often turns out that it's mainly people working a few flexi-hours so they can vary their start and finish times within a relatively small window. What people aren't doing are any of the bolder types of flex, such as a compressed work week or job sharing. It is often the case that people are looking for more flex options than are currently available. The uptake of the different types of flex will give you some insight about whether or not that is happening for people in your team. Measuring a combination of flex uptake and perception is a powerful combination if you want to assess the risk or opportunity of flex in your team. That's when the third and final measure of flex perception becomes really helpful.

Perception: Flex and its perception

How are people feeling about flexible work? Is it delivering on their expectations?

People make decisions about their work based on how they feel. If you want to attract and retain the right people in your team for longer and see them do their best work, then it's important to track how they feel flex is working for them, or not. I often ask people the question, "How well is flex going for you and your team right now?" and ask for a score out of 10. The spread as well as the average of that score is a good metric by which to gauge the perception of flex. You can track this regularly and look at it in the context of the other two parts of the flex measures triangle to tell a powerful story that can drive where you take flex next.

Case study

A large organisation conducted a survey to measure the work-life balance of its employees, including the use of flexible work. A few years earlier they had adopted a bolder flex policy giving greater permission to people to work beyond the traditional model of nine to five, as part of its inclusive work practices. In this survey, the uptake of flex was reported at 78 per cent, which seemed great cause for celebration. The policy was working in practice!

However, digging a little deeper into the numbers, a different story emerged. Some 73 per cent of those people already working flexibly wanted access to additional flexible work options. And what about the people not working flexibly? Was that out of choice? Did they like the traditional nine to five? No, not at all – 81 per cent of those working the traditional pattern wanted to have some form of flex, but for some reason weren't getting it.

All up, this amounted to three in four people who weren't getting the form of flex they wanted, whether they were already working flexibly or not. Their story illustrates why measuring the impact of flex is so important. If we put a policy out there that we think is permissive, it might not actually be landing that way in practice. It takes some thoughtful measures to track whether or not flex is actually landing the way you want it to.

> What would people in your team and organisation report back in a survey like this one?

Key ingredient 2
Flex **leadership** style

The second ingredient that will fuel your flex maturity is the right leadership style. Leadership is one of those factors that can accelerate or completely undermine the way flex plays out in practice in our teams and organisations. If I had a dollar for every time someone told me that their flex depends on their manager, I could retire tomorrow!

Flex leadership style is not just about the flexible work decisions you make for people in your team; how you role model and talk about flex counts. People are pattern seekers. If they see a consistent pattern of behaviour, messages and decisions from you, they will feel better able to predict what you think about or expect from a flex arrangement. If there are inconsistencies, people will see them and won't feel able to trust that flex is something they can rely on or make full use of, which will curtail the benefits for you and your team.

Is your leadership style working for, or counterproductive to, flex in your team?

Leadership categories

I see three categories of flex leadership in the work I do:

1. Pro-flex

2. Flex-hesitant

3. Flex-averse

Although pro-flex leadership is what you want to aim for, all three have their positive and shadow sides. These descriptions help you to consider how your leadership style impacts on flex for your team and others in your organisation.

Leadership category 1: **Pro-flex**

Positive traits

The pro-flex leader is usually someone with a growth mindset. They like new ideas and often have high-trust, engaged teams. They are skilled at creating an environment where people can do their best work. A people-focused leader, first and foremost.

Shadow side

They often jump to 'yes' to flex before they have worked through the broader implications and impact of a flexible work arrangement. They forget to test the readiness or practicality of a flex arrangement on others. This creates a sense of fragility in flexible work arrangements because they are unsupported or unsustainable and need to be reworked to find a solution that everyone is able to work with. The pro-flex leader sometimes risks their own burnout in an attempt to create a flexible work environment for everyone else in their team.

Leadership category 2: **Flex-hesitant**

Positive traits

The flex-hesitant leader is someone who often has a growth mindset. They tend to be very experienced and skilled people leaders, have a good reputation for delivery and get good results. The decisions they make will often be well thought through, workable and minimise disruption to delivery and other colleagues or customers.

Shadow side

Hesitancy often comes from a sole focus on delivery that crowds out exploring how flex could lead to higher levels of performance, productivity and wellbeing. They see the risks flex poses to their reputation for delivery and getting work done in a way that they know works well already. These concerns can lead to paralysis or minimal, incremental and conservative flex decisions. Ultimately, team members leave in pursuit of a manager who offers more flex scope.

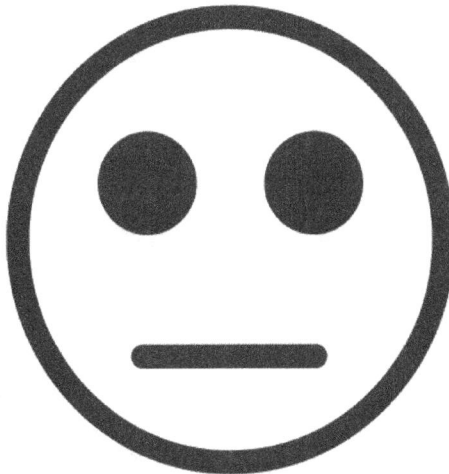

Leadership category 3: **Flex-averse**

Positive traits

The flex-averse leader values certainty and offers that to the people in their team about how, when and where work gets done. Members of the team know how they can work together and there is very little flex complexity to deal with. Certainty matters to them. They know how they like to work and find that the disruption to their preferred way of working creates anxiety and fear of loss of control. Flex is granted to people by exception, not as a rule.

Shadow side

Flex-averse leaders focus on the barriers of flex rather than the potential opportunities. They have often been burnt by flex going wrong in the past and don't want to repeat that experience. They miss out on the benefits of flex and won't be able to attract and retain people to work in their team in the longer term. Team cohesion suffers due to high turnover.

Reflection questions

You:
- Which flex leadership style most closely fits you at the moment?

- What other flex leadership styles do you observe in your organisation?

- What are the positive impacts of your flex leadership style?

- What are the negative consequences of your flex leadership style?

Others:
- How is the dominant flex leadership style shaping the maturity level in your organisation?

- How can you encourage other leaders to explore and develop their flex style?

Key ingredient 3
Reliable **tools** and practice

The third key ingredient to fuelling flex maturity is through reliable tools, practice and support. The Flex-Team Toolkit is designed to give you everything you need to fuel a positive experience and impact, shifting you ever closer to becoming a flexpert organisation feeling comfortable on new and solid ground.

The details of the main, core flex-team tools are covered in Chapters 6 and 7. Here you'll find out how to have regular, proactive team-based flex discussions, at least every six months, as well as use common tools and language across the team.

Top tip

Check out the Flex-Team Toolkit Index in the appendix. It's a quick-reference guide to everything in the toolkit. It also high-lights which of the tools and downloads are core to the success of flex in your team and which are optional for you to use when the time is right or when a specific need arises.

Something missing?

Like a three-legged stool, it takes all three ingredients to stand up and mature your flexible work practice: **Strategy**, **Leadership**, and **Tools**.

When you only have two out of three you'll find it wobbling at best, or collapsing at worst. Here's what happens if one of the three ingredients is missing.

Hesitant: missing strong connection to strategy

In the absence of a strong connection to strategy, flexible work feels like the trendy idea, or the flavour of the month. It's here for now, but there's little trust that it is reliably here for the longer term. There's little visibility or clarity about the purpose it serves for the organisation and why it matters to the decision makers at the top. People often perceive that it's given begrudgingly, rather than proactively part of a workforce strategy that is coherent and supports the organisation's long-term and strategic goals. This leads teams to hesitate in trying bigger, bolder flexible work ideas, investing in better enablers for flexible work or fully embedding their flexible work practice. They perceive a risk that it might all be rolled back at short notice.

Inconsistent: missing pro-flex leadership

When there is a mix of flex-leadership styles across the organisation your flexible work approach is driven more by the comfort level of the manager than by anything else. If I'm lucky enough to have a manager who is pro-flex then I'm going to get more opportunities to benefit from working flexibly. If my manager changes that is going to feel under threat. As I look across the organisation this shows up as inconsistencies that are hard to justify. The flexibility people have access to has little to do with the work they do or what they need. Everyone can clearly see which managers are more pro-flex and who isn't based on what's available or normal in each team. This inconsistency is obvious to everyone. Those without access to flex feel resentful and those who do don't trust that it is here to stay.

Dissonant: missing flex-tools and support

If people are not given the right tools and support to get the best from flex, they feel frustrated and let down. People become cynical about the dissonance between pro-flex messaging and the level of practical support to bring the intent to life. This is often referred to as flex-washing. Flex-washing is when the rhetoric of flex doesn't stack up in practice. If people hear messages about why flex is important and managers telling them to be bold and try new ideas, but no-one offers any practical tools and support to get there, the dissonance becomes the focus, rather than the potential benefits and pay-offs from flex.

Chapter summary

- Flexible work expectations have accelerated since the pandemic.
- Flexible work is in a fragile state.
- To fuel your team towards a new normal, you'll need a clear connection to strategy, pro-flex leadership, plus new tools and practice.
- Connection to strategy involves consistent leadership messaging and impact measures.
- Leadership requires a pro-flex approach with new tools that are fit for purpose.
- New tools and practice need to be used across the team at least every six months and commonly used in every team across the organisation.
- It takes all three of these ingredients to move past the fragile state and fuel your team to new and solid ground.

Chapter 2 notes

1   www.buffer.com/state-of-remote-work/2022
2   https://.gartner.com/en/articles/employees-seek-personal-value-and-purpose-at-work-be-prepared-to- deliver?source=BLD-200123&utm_medium=social&utm_source=bambu&utm_campaign=SM_GB_YOY_ GTR_SOC_BU1_SM-BA-SWG

"Hybrid, if it's well-organized,
I think it's a win-win."

Nick Bloom, *Business Insider*

Chapter 3

Flex challenges

You can be forgiven for feeling like flexible work is a bit of a hoax. There is so much buzz around proclaiming the wonders of flexibility, including a lot of commentary telling us how we should have been doing this sooner and faster with questions about why it has taken a pandemic for us to see the light.

What I see happening with flex is that it's going wrong about as often as it's going right. The good news is, you're not the problem. Well, even if you're some of the problem, it's definitely not all on you and you are absolutely not alone.

There are common scenarios playing out that we will look at in this chapter so you can see how you and your team are faring. There are also some common challenges that people are experiencing. After the disruption and accelerated uptake of flex from the pandemic, there were always going to be some teething problems. We can use these individual and collective experiences to guide us towards how flex can evolve for the better. This chapter gives you some insight into what's going wrong and what's challenging. You'll be pleased to discover that you'll find ways to resolve the issues when they crop up, or even know what to look out for to avoid the challenges, before they get in the way.

Flexible work as a win-win

To know when flex isn't working well, we first need to consider what good looks like. Only then can we determine if it's failing to live up to one or more of our many expectations.

Ideally, flexible work is at its best when both the employer and the employee are getting what they perceive to be a 'win' from the arrangement. The term win-win has become overused, and is often fraught with untested assumptions about what both parties actually want. Let's start by outlining the assumptions clearly so you can approach them wide-eyed and ready to explore in your flex-team discussions (outlined in detail in Chapters 6 and 7).

The 'win' employer perspective

From an employer's point of view, the highest priority when it comes to flex is that the work gets done. That is the perspective built into this map (on page 60). It's true that there are other important priorities too, from an employer perspective, such as having a productive and healthy workforce who are sustained in the long term.

In this section I've simplified the employer perspective to a 'work delivery' focus so we can see the danger of it and the damage that can be done if we don't couple that with a longer-term view to include the priority of wellbeing.

Employers are deeply concerned about burnout, and no employer I've worked with would ever consider burnout as a 'win'. However, what's actually happening is that burnout is on the rise after the experience of the pandemic[1] and the media coverage of The Great Resignation has caught the interest of many of us. People are choosing to leave their jobs in search of work that will give them a better quality of life and is less likely to do them harm.

Many employers are still grappling with how to combine delivery with a sustained, healthy workforce in the context of more flexible work demands. It's in this context that I have created the flex scenario map to highlight the pitfalls of an employer taking a myopic, short-term, delivery-at-all-costs perspective.

The 'win' employee perspective

From an employee's point of view, you want to have some choices available that help you to be at your best whether you're focusing on work or on other important aspects of your life. This is about finding ways to do your work that at least sustains, or even lifts, your wellbeing.

Amartyr Sen, who I referred to in the introduction, is considered the founding father of wellbeing economics. He is an economist, philosopher and Nobel Laureate who developed the capability approach to wellbeing.

The essence of the capability approach to wellbeing is freedom to choose. The freedom for people to 'be' and 'do' the things that they value and have reason to value. This access to choice – true access to choice – is central in Sen's work.

If that is how wellbeing is fostered in each of us, there are two important implications. One is good news and the other is more of a mixed bag.

The first is that no-one else can tell you what you need or what is best for your wellbeing. The reason for that is because they won't understand the depth of what you value and have reason to value. They won't know your history, where your values have come from and what experiences shaped them. This means that as managers, we have to move away from rules and paternalism. We really don't know what is best for others. Rules, even when they are well intended, are highly likely to backfire and get in the way of someone being able to get the 'win' they need for their personal wellbeing. We touch again on rules in Chapter 6, but I will say here that the common, yet limiting, rules I see often look like, "No more than two days working from home per week", or, "Core work hours must be 9.30am to 2.30pm."

The second implication is that if you're the only one who can really know the answer to the question, "What do you need to be at your best?" then you'll need to do the work to find out what the answer is.

I find that one of the hardest questions in the world is, "What do you want?" So many of us are unpractised when it comes to knowing what we need or what we want. We know when things are wrong, because we experience a negative emotional response, but knowing where to go from there is not always easy, or obvious. Having tools to help people work out their preferences when it comes to choices about when and where to work can be really helpful. It won't deliver the perfect fit every time, but it will narrow down the scope and give people space to experiment with options that are more likely to give them a wellbeing boost.

In the same way that the employer's priority is artificially constrained to 'work delivery', the employee's priority is constrained to wellbeing. This isn't how many of us approach work in reality. You'll know what it feels like when you're working at your best – you're in flow and highly productive. It's a great feeling. Employees want to feel like that more often. But they don't want to deliver at the expense of their wellbeing. For the purposes of highlighting the pitfalls of undervaluing delivery, this map looks at the scenarios that play out when the key priority for employees is solely their own wellbeing.

Case study

I was running a workshop and a manager in the room proudly told me that he tells his team off if any of them work past 6pm or answer emails at the weekend. He felt that it was part of his duty of care to make sure that people switched off and didn't feel obliged to work more than their agreed hours.

I opened up the discussion to the rest of the room when I noticed some uncomfortable shifting in chairs from some of his colleagues. Another manager said there were people in his team who preferred to work later in the evening – to catch up on their emails when most people have finished for the day. This also meant they could take a couple of hours in the late afternoon to pick up their children from school and make the family dinner without the need for childcare or a feeling of guilt. A couple of others in the room agreed, some preferring to work later sometimes, or to clear emails on a Sunday night so they could start later on Monday mornings.

The first manager thought about it and realised that his "6pm cut off" rule might not work well for everyone. When I asked him what he'd prefer to try instead, he decided to talk to his team about the rules after the workshop, and let them inform his next step.

Scenarios: the good, the bad and the ugly

Take a look at the map below. It outlines the main scenarios playing out right now when it comes to flexible work. You will probably recognise them and be able to categorise some situations you've been in, or have observed.

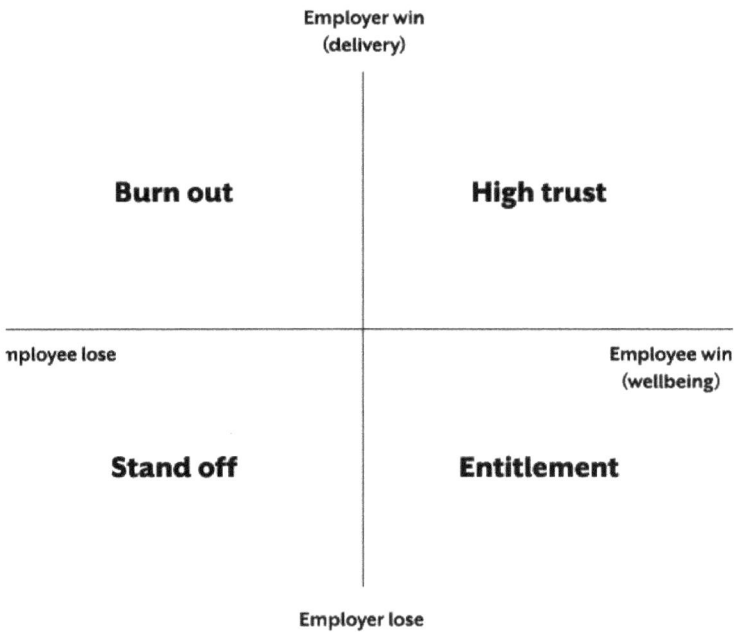

Employer win
(delivery)

Burn out   **High trust**

nployee lose   Employee win
                                          (wellbeing)

Stand off   **Entitlement**

Employer lose

Let's explore the four scenarios in the map:

1. High trust
The good

2. Entitlement
The bad

3. Burnout
The bad

4. Stand off
The ugly

Scenario 1
High trust: *the good*

When flexible work goes well, everyone gets more of what they need. The ideal, utopic state of flex that we are all in search of is this one. What this takes is for both parties to be clear with each other about what their version of 'win' means and how both can be served well. This moves us out of the myopic state from each party and into a shared and clear understanding about how we get more of both.

When both parties are getting more of what they need, trust in each other, as well as trust in the flexible work process, grows. We need to be able to be credible in what we say and follow that up with responsible action. We also need to feel supported and able to share and disclose things about ourselves and our work with others in the team. These aspects of building trust are all components of the trust quotient, or trust equation, outlined in *The Trusted Advisor*. Focusing only on our own needs undermines that trust and is what we explore in the 'entitlement' scenario next.

The tools in this book are designed to help you get there and stay there, perpetuating a culture of high trust.

At its simplest, it's a process of being clear about what delivery looks like, as well as being clear about what personal work preferences are and using the overlap of those two things to come up with feasible flexible work options.

Chapter 6 has everything your team members need to do that work and keep it up to date.

Scenario 2
Entitlement: *the bad*

There are two 'bad' scenarios to explore. The first is what I call 'entitlement'. When a person has a narrow view of their delivery expectations they can be perceived as making flexible work choices that are selfish or entitled. Most of the time this happens not by malicious intent, but because someone doesn't fully appreciate their wider contribution and who they have obligations to.

The best way to avoid getting here with someone in your team, or to find your way out of here, is to use the 'Delivery' tools in Chapter 6. The Landscape of Expectations and the Delivery First templates help people to explore and reset the full scope of their delivery expectations. Once those are clear and agreed then the person is safe to explore flexible work options within those boundaries. That's how they can move back into the 'high trust' quadrant.

Case study

I was talking to a manager in an engineering business about the challenges she was experiencing with flex. She was supportive of flexible work and a positive role model to other engineers, having built a successful career while also working part-time and flexibly.

One of her direct reports, Sasha, was making full use of flex, but it wasn't working. Sasha's engineering role was part-time for three days per week. This gave her time and money to pursue her passion for live music performance. She was fitting her engineering role around everything else she valued in her life, which in principle her manager supported. However, the choices Sasha made about the hours she worked were entirely opposite to those of everyone else she connected with. She was rarely available to talk to clients or to discuss her projects' progress with colleagues. She felt this was OK because she could answer emails in the early hours of the morning or late at night.

What people needed sometimes, and weren't getting, was timely input from her at critical points in the project. This was causing substantial delays and frustration across the team. She'd slipped into the entitled quadrant without realising it. When the manager discussed it with her as part of a regular catch up, she hadn't noticed the impact her hours of work were having on her colleagues. Sasha wanted to be more challenged in the work she was being given. In the discussion, her manager explained that Sasha was capable of doing more, and that taking on more responsibility would need to involve more collaboration with others in the team. They discussed the options to move forward and agreed there needed to be some overlap between Sasha's hours and those of others in the team to support their workflow as well as Sasha's professional development goals.

Scenario 3
Burnout: *the bad*

This scenario is the most common of the two 'bad' options that I observe in my work. There are two sub-scenarios to the 'burnout' quadrant. The first is 'flexibility gratitude'. I often find that people keep working just because it's possible, not because it's a good idea. When people feel grateful for the flexibility to work hours that fit around their life and from a location of their choice, they want to show that they are committed and grateful. To demonstrate this commitment and gratitude to their employer they fail to commit to work-home boundaries and rarely switch off.

The other version of this is when a person is in 'overwhelm'. They might even be perceived as being in the 'entitlement' quadrant, but actually they have too much on their delivery plate. The expectations stack up to more than they are able to meet. It's not that they're unaware of expectations, it's that the expectations are too high and are in need of a reset. In a 'fragile' flex maturity stage, as described in Chapter 2, the organisational culture is often one that values short-term delivery with high levels of manager accountability. In this state, it's easy for people to find themselves in 'overwhelm' because they want to contribute and what that can look like at its most extreme is 'getting stuff done' at all costs.

To help people get out of the 'flexibility gratitude' state they can turn to the 'Personal Preferences' tools in Chapter 6. You can work with them to make sure they're considering what they need in order to be at their best and sustain their energy over the longer term.

To help people get out of the 'overwhelm' scenario they need both the 'Delivery' tools as well as the 'Personal Preferences' tools. Many managers I work with don't feel they always know until it's too late that a team member has found themselves in 'overwhelm'. With the lower levels of visibility available in a more flexible work environment, it's harder for managers to spot the classic signs of overwhelm. In many cases the person feeling overwhelmed feels it's their fault and makes efforts to hide the situation from their team or manager.

The tools in Chapter 6 are designed to cover all bases so that anyone, whether they're hiding their 'overwhelm' or not, has a regular check in about how their delivery and personal preferences are stacking up. This makes it much less likely that people in your teams will continue to stay in or slip into any of these unfavourable flex scenarios. The flex-team tools in Chapter 6 become a default for everyone in your team, including yourself. That way you avoid the 'bad' situations and instead maintain 'high trust' for everyone to get a win-win.

Scenario 4
Stand off: *the ugly*

This is where you really don't want to end up. It's the 'ugly' scenario for a reason. This is the place you go to with your team members when they've spent too long in either 'entitlement' or 'burnout'. There's been no supportive intervention until eventually something (or someone) breaks. When this happens the employment relationship reaches a point of stand off and it can break down entirely.

In the entitlement scenario, left unchecked, the resentment from others builds and eventually their working relationships break down. The person might experience exclusion, passive-aggressive behaviour from colleagues or an all-out, aggressively direct accusation of entitlement. When colleagues feel that they are filling the gaps left behind by someone they perceive to be a selfish team member, it won't end well unless it's dealt with and resolved quickly.

In the burnout scenario, eventually the person realises that the way they are working is unsustainable. If that isn't reset, or they don't know how to reset, they will eventually decide they can't carry on that way and will choose to find an alternative work option that won't be harmful to their wellbeing.

Which scenarios do you see?

All four of these scenarios are playing out in every workplace.
You can use this tool to map where you think people are within your own team. It can help you decide which tools you want to focus on first to help keep the centre of gravity in 'high trust'.

The main challenges with flex

In the work I do, I ask people what their number one challenge is with flexible work. I ask this to find out what's getting in the way of flex being the best it can be in their workplace. It's a useful question that you can use too when you have your regular flex-team discussions, as outlined in Chapter 5. It can become part of your regular monitoring practice to measure the impact of flex. The insights you'll get will help you take action and keep flex moving forward positively for you, your team and others you connect with.

This is a summary of the results I had from asking this question of my clients. The people who responded were a mix of senior leaders, managers and team members.

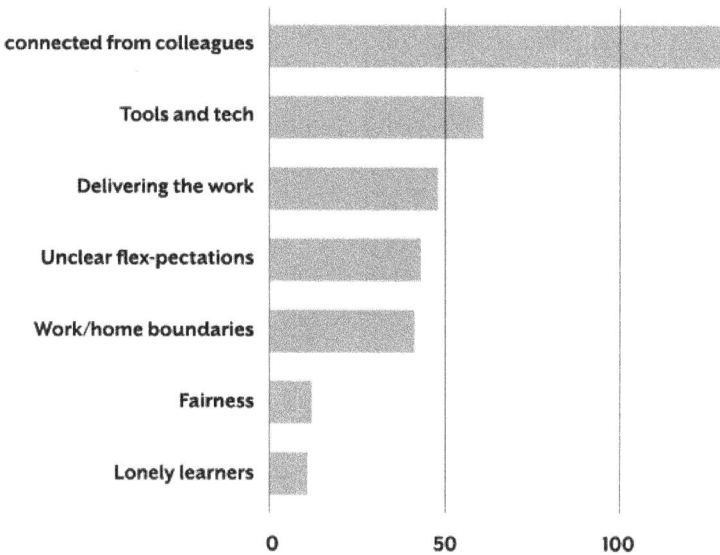

Flex challenges

I'll go through each of these challenges so you can recognise them if or when they present themselves in your flex-team discussions. I'll also sign post you to the flex-team tools that will help you navigate your way out of these common challenges.

Flex challenge 1
Disconnected from colleagues

This is by far the biggest challenge people are facing when it comes to flex. It plays out in a number of ways, but it's all about how we connect with each other and how much harder it has become since we embraced more flexible and hybrid working.

People miss being able to rely on a busy office, full of people who are there at the same time. It is no longer our default work environment. It used to be an easy way for us to stay connected with each other without having to work hard for it. Well, it used to be easy for those who worked in the traditional, full-time work pattern. It was always a challenge for those who worked outside of it, such as part-time employees. Now we are all much more appreciative of the challenge that those people faced.

We all now miss being able to find the right person to ask a quick question to, or being able to get expert support from a colleague in a timely way to help us keep moving forward with our workflow. We also miss the informal, unplanned conversations and connections, whether it's purely social, or those unplanned chats about our work that lead to new ideas and insights about new and different work that might ultimately follow. This is getting in the way of the promised productivity benefits we have come to expect from flexible work.

In a hybrid workplace, this issue of disconnection is going to be our biggest obstacle.

Nick Bloom, a Professor of Economics at Stanford University, has been studying this in depth. He predicts that a typical five-day working week of Monday to Friday will shift to a hybrid pattern of two to three days at home, and two to three days in the office.[2] The most likely days at home will be Mondays and Fridays, with Tuesday to Thursday in the office. The days in the office will be focused much more deliberately on these connections, collaboration and creativity. This leaves the book-ends of the week to crack on with the quiet work that we all need to get through without distraction. This style of work arrangement requires planning, cooperation and structure. It won't just happen without us being deliberate about it.

Following on from a podcast conversation[3] Nick Bloom had after some work he did on hybrid work back in March 2021, I started thinking about the hybrid workplace and its productivity benefits in this way.

Hybrid productivity

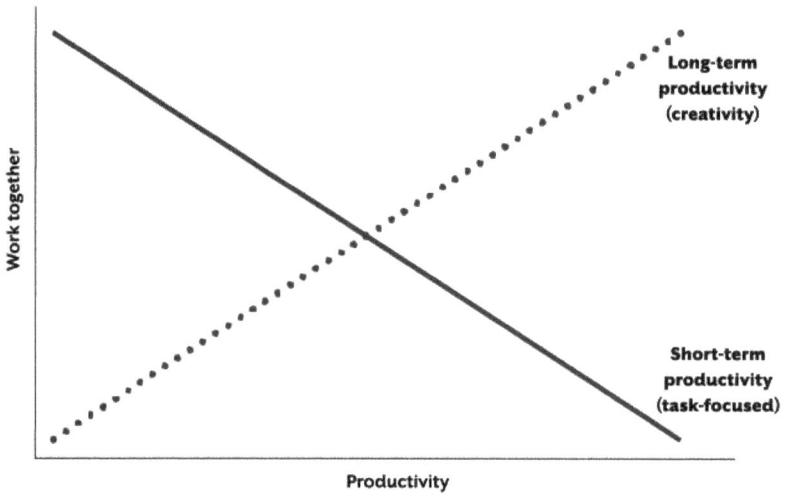

What this shows is that when we work alone, either at home or in a quiet space in the office, we have a high level of short-term productivity. There is a lot of productivity benefit to be gained from reducing the distractions we regularly gift each other when we're all working in the same place at the same time. This short-term productivity benefit is about efficiency, or doing known and familiar tasks in a shorter amount of time.

The cost of over-focusing on this type of productivity is that we miss working with our colleagues. That disconnection so many of us are being challenged by is actually an important driver of our creativity and long-term productivity.

If short-term productivity is about efficiency, doing the same things faster, then long-term productivity is about getting creative, testing new ideas and ultimately evolving what we do in our work. This is when we let go of old tasks, because they've been upgraded by something else.

We replace former tasks with new and different work that is ultimately of higher value than the old stuff.

This is what we miss when we're feeling disconnected. We're missing the chance to be at our most creative and get our brains working beyond an immediate job and into the realm of possibility.

If your team is going to be experimenting with 'place' as one of its flexible variables, then consider the impact of that for both short-term and long-term productivity. Sharing this with your team as they design how they want to work will encourage them to find ways of keeping their connections strong, as well as how to involve other people outside the team who are important to the work they do.

To support that, look at the 'Delivery' tools in Chapter 6.

Flex challenge 2
Tools and technology

Many people are learning through experience that their tools and technology both in the office and at home aren't yet ideal. This can be the
quality of the wifi connections, the equipment they have access to, such
as desk space or a monitor, or software and online collaboration tools.

In Chapter 7, I show you how to explore the enablers, or disablers,
of flexible work. This is more about 'how' the team works flexibly rather
than 'what' the flexible work arrangements are. Flexible work enablers
fall into the categories of tools, technology and team commitments.

Flex challenge 3
Delivering the work

Often it's the constraints from the work itself that present barriers to flexible work. I find that people experience this in two different ways. The first is from the sheer volume of delivery and the pressure they feel. This manifests as a perception that flex is a luxury they cannot afford without letting the team down. This is back to the 'burnout' quadrant described earlier, when someone is in the 'overwhelm' situation. The tools in Chapter 6 bring these people the reset they need. They get delivery back into a sustainable place as well as understanding their own wellbeing needs. On that basis they move forward with a work arrangement that offers both productivity and wellbeing benefits that persist over the longer term.

The other driver of this challenge is when the way in which the work is delivered is fixed to a particular time or place. The tier one workforce described in the introduction is often in this situation. I work with teams for whom these constraints are very real. What I remind them of is to focus on what they can flex, what is possible, rather than what isn't. When they look at the hours, days or place variables that have some flex opportunities they often get creative pretty quickly. For example, they might think of a variation to their existing roster system that gives them more favourable options for the hours or days of work. These teams find new ways of working that give them more productivity and wellbeing benefits, particularly in the short term. After a while, they also start having conversations about the systems they're using, the constraints they face today, and test the assumption that these things are fixed in the longer term. This is when they level-up again and look at new delivery options that will provide even greater levels of flexibility in the future.

Case study

One team I worked with were still using a paper-based system. They needed signatures from senior leaders on hard-copy papers on a regular basis. This constrained them in terms of place of work, but also in terms of when, because their hours and days needed to mirror those of the senior leaders. What they noticed was that as more senior leaders worked from home once or twice per week, they needed to have an alternative option. They set up leaders with electronic signatures and asked the IT team to upgrade their paper system to a secure online version. Once this new way of working was in place, it made a huge difference to their flexible work options.

Flex challenge 4
Unclear flex-pectations

As described in Chapter 2, the fragile state that many organisations are in right now shows up with many people feeling unsure of what's OK and what isn't when it comes to flex arrangements. This can be through the absence of one or more of the three key ingredients: strategy, leadership, and tools.

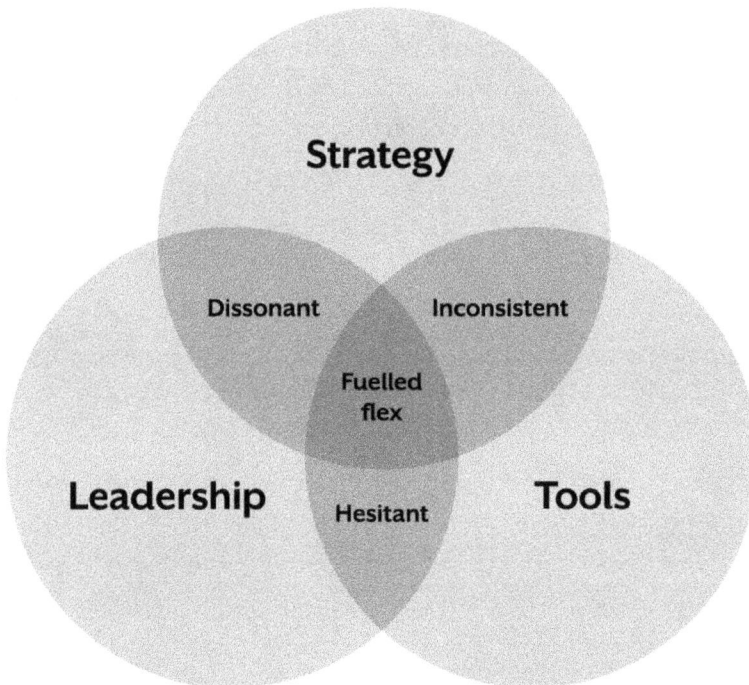

When the expectations of flex are unclear and uncertain, this triggers a fear response in people. This fear crowds out the psychological safety that you and your team need to feel safe enough to experiment with flex. Often, the benefits come from testing and learning from these flex experiments agreed at your flex-team discussions.

The tools in Chapter 6 will provide you and your team with enough structure to feel safe enough to try out some new flexible ways of working.

Your pro-flex leadership style as described in Chapter 2 will give the team confidence that you're with them as they experiment with different ideas, measuring and monitoring the impact as you go.

The more you can connect flex to the strategic goals of the organisation, the clearer people will be about why this matters. This is another confidence boost as they work through the flex-team tools with their colleagues. If this isn't as clear as it could be, pointing that out to senior leaders you work with and the risk that it carries can help get the message through loud and clear if it's not quite there yet.

Flex challenge 5
Work-home boundaries

Many people are now working from home regularly. Most of us who now fall into the 'hybrid' or 'remote' tiers of the workforce used to only work from home on rare and ad hoc occasions. Previously it was reserved for situations such as a tradesperson coming to the house to fix something, or needing to work from home for a half-day before going to our child's sports day in the afternoon.

Now that working from home is more prevalent and is likely to stay that way, people find it hard to establish healthy boundaries between work and home. When work and home domains were in geographically different places, it was easier to do. Technology often blurred those boundaries, as mobile communications followed us wherever we went, but the pressure to blur them is higher when work and home life all happen in the same physical space on a regular basis.

The 'Managing Boundaries' tool in Chapter 6 is the best way to help people struggling with this challenge. It helps them identify their boundary preferences and then test that against their reality. If the gap between preference and reality is high, that's a sure sign that this is a critical challenge for them right now and will be having a detrimental impact on their wellbeing.

Flex challenge 6
Fairness

Fairness challenges are most often fuelled by the equity conundrum managers feel when faced with flexible work requests, as described in Chapter 5. When you're at the centre of the flexible work complexity, you have all the control but not enough timely information to make the best decisions. Taking yourself out of the centre and facilitating and participating in regular, proactive flex-team discussions is the single biggest gift you can give yourself and the team. Coupling that move away from the centre with the tools in Chapters 6 and 7 will get you and the team into the high-trust, win-win quadrant. The place where everyone wants to be.

Flex challenge 7
Lonely learners

New starters in your team and people who have recently been promoted into a bigger, stretching role, often find themselves struggling to learn as quickly as they used to.

Until recently, a lot of growth happened informally. Something inter-esting pops up. It's unplanned, unexpected and full of learning oppor-tunities for someone in the team. You, or the person's buddy or mentor, would spot the learning opportunity and share it in the moment, or as early as possible.

With so many of us now spending more time working remotely or at different times from each other, those 'learning moments' have a lot more friction. You can't simply pop over to the person and say, "Hey, I think you'll find this really interesting …" Instead, we need to build in these development opportunities with flex in mind.

With some deliberate planning there are various good ways to get the best of both flexible work and learning.

This tool provides a light structure to help alleviate the problems faced by lonely learners in your team.

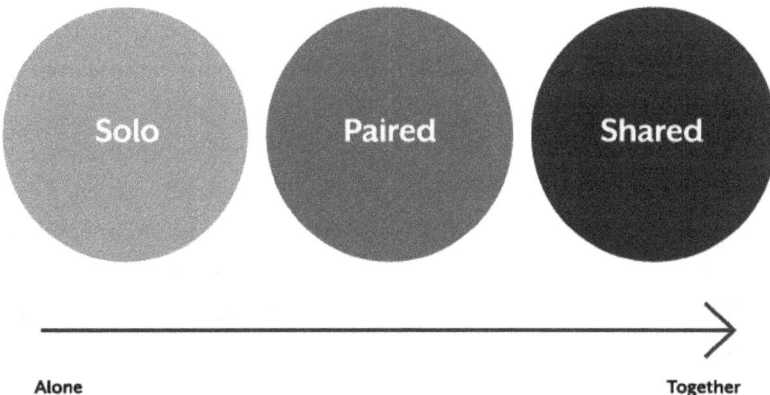

Solo   Paired   Shared

Alone   Together

When you're having a development conversation with someone in your team, this tool is a useful supplement. Start by asking each person to consider their development goals and how that learning will best happen. Use these three categories of solo, paired and shared learning to identify who else needs to be involved to support their development.

Solo

What can they do by themselves that gives them a stretch? What will they feel empowered by if they're given a chance to try on their own? What formal learning can they get stuck into when they have quiet time working from home?

Paired

How can they pair up with others who can coach and mentor them, whether in-person or virtually? Who can they have a peer coaching arrangement with? Is there someone at a similar career point to them who could mutually benefit? What kind of mentor do they need right now? What support do they need from you in the form of one-to-ones? How can this paired learning be scheduled into the working week so you know it's happening?

Shared

What team-time can you build into the schedule so that those opportunities for unplanned, unscheduled learning can still take place? What commitments will others make to pick up the phone when they're working remotely, despite the added friction, and bring in the learner to meetings and discussions that they can learn a lot from?

Once everyone has taken the time to explore what their development needs are and who they need to connect with, you can bring this into your regular flex-team discussions. Professional development then becomes part of the delivery discussion, which is covered more broadly in Chapter 6. Here you explore how to manage delivery and development as a team.

Everyone wins when their development is supported and they can support the development of those around them.

Chapter summary

- Flexible work is going wrong about as often as it's going right.
- The best-case scenario is when everyone gets a win: trust builds in the team and in the process.
- The scenarios to avoid can be summarised as **'burnout'**, **'entitlement'** and **'stand off'**.
- There are common challenges people are facing with flexible work.
- The challenges, in order of significance, are:

  » disconnected from colleagues
  » tools and technology
  » delivering the work
  » unclear flex-pectations
  » work-home boundaries
  » fairness
  » lonely learners.

Chapter 3 notes

1   www.linkedin.com/posts/dr-jarrod-haar-phd-frsnz-cfhrnz-55776230_using-our-summer-break-to-combat-burnout-activity-6871959470331850752-Ydkc?utm_source=linkedin_share&utm_medium=member

2   https://siepr.stanford.edu/publications/policy-brief/hybrid-future-work

3   www.cheerfulpodcast.com/rtbc-episodes/zoom-where-it-happens-building-a-digital-society-for-all

"If I had an hour to solve a problem I'd spend 55 minutes thinking about the problem and 5 minutes thinking about solutions."

Albert Einstein

Chapter 4

Masquerading flex issues

A number of issues are often misdiagnosed as flexible work problems. I refer to them as masquerading flex issues because the underlying cause is something else. Flexible work simply exacerbates that underlying problem and can become the victim of an attempt to ease the pain.

Resource constraints

Not having enough people in the team to cover the work that needs to be delivered doesn't go away when you overlay flexible work. It's like having a patchwork quilt that doesn't have enough patches to cover the bed. It doesn't matter how you arrange them, you simply don't have enough pieces.

Flexible work is well researched for its productivity gains. People can often get their work done within less time. Rather than create idle time for thumb twiddling, this capacity is often just enough to free themselves up for doing better-quality work on a project that hasn't been going anywhere for the last six months, or finding time for professional development. It's not a way of creating significant new capacity in your team or an opportunity to intensify work by giving them more to do. When teams are working flexibly, especially with people working part-time, you will often need additional resources to make up the full-time contingent of your team, such as employing an extra part-time person.

Under-performance

In any circumstances, having someone in the team under-performing is hard work as a manager. Flexible work is another layer of complexity when managing a performance issue. Flex isn't the core of the problem. In fact, research shows a positive relationship between flexible work and individual performance.[1]

Like any good performance management process, setting clear and shared expectations is the place to begin. The 'Delivery' tools in Chapter 6 will be really helpful to spend some time working through together, especially if performance has been an issue in the past.

It is also important to enable the person to make good choices about the best way for them to get their work done. This is where the 'Wellbeing' tools can be really helpful. Test and learn what works well and have regular conversations as part of the performance process. Check in more frequently than the regular, six-monthly flex-team discussion. Use these tools on a tighter timeframe alongside the performance management process until you both feel that performance is up to scratch.

Culture of 'delivery at all costs'

Similar to resource constraints, if the work expected of the team is more than can be sustainably delivered, flex can add further complexity and stress to the situation. Organisations at the 'fragile' flex maturity stage often have a culture that places a high value on delivery. This drives high levels of expectations for you and your team, which can sometimes become *too* high.

Flex isn't the problem here, it's the culture of relentless delivery or the dark side of 'heroism' that needs to be examined. We all know that sometimes we are willing and able to go the extra mile when our organisations need it. Those moments of high pressure that require a short-term push to get through. There are organisations that find themselves with this level of expectation as their default, rather than the exception.

In this environment, flex can feel impossible. Under these conditions, people are pushed into the 'burnout' quadrant and it's not a sustainable place to be. People have the means to keep working and are expected to do so, but that doesn't mean it's a good idea. If there isn't a way into the high-trust, win-win quadrant, then many people at some point will find themselves reflecting on what they need from a workplace and choose to go elsewhere, with or without the relationship intact.

Challenging that culture as a manager somewhere in the middle of the hierarchy can feel deeply uncomfortable. By highlighting and discussing with your peers and senior leaders the three key ingredients that shift the maturity from fragile to fuelled (Strategy, Leadership, Tools) you'll find that you're able to start shifting it, slowly but surely. In the meantime, doing what you can with your team using the tools in this book will help you make the most of what's possible and get the best from flex, even if it has its limitations for now.

Chapter summary

- There are a handful of issues commonly misdiagnosed as problems with flex.
- Resource constraints: not having enough people to do the work required is often perceived as a problem with the flex work arrangements of the people in the team.
- Under-performance: if someone is under-performing in their role, flex isn't the core problem. Flex has been shown to have a positive relationship with individual performance.
- 'Delivery-at-all-costs' culture: similar to resource constraints. If the work expected is more than can be sustainably delivered, flex can add further complexity and stress to the situation.

Chapter 4 notes

1   Working Families and Cranfield University 2009 *Flexible Working and Performance, Summary of Research, Working Families*

Part 2

Get the best from flex

"Flexible work is the future (and the future is here)."

Tracy Brower, *Forbes*

Chapter 5

Flex teams

Flex for the few

Historically, flexible work was used to enable people with caring responsibilities to continue to do their existing job.

Typically, flexible work gave new mothers a pathway back to work after parental leave, and the ability to juggle the demands of family life alongside their job with a bit more wriggle room than would otherwise be available. Flexible work is often part of a diversity strategy for organisations trying to level the playing field for more women to find their way beyond the glass ceiling, particularly in leadership roles.

We have a long way to go to encourage all parents, regardless of gender, to feel willing and able to flex their work to fit around the caring responsibilities they have, or would like to have. There is a growing number of working dads working more flexibly. Part of the reason I love doing this work is to make flexibility more widely available to more groups of people who have been left behind.

Case study

When a couple I know, both experienced professionals in separate organisations, started their family, the dad asked his manager if he could work part-time, four days per week, to help balance the childcare responsibilities with his partner. The request was declined because he was considered too new to the team to be able to manage the demands of the job and build the relationships he needed in anything less than five days a week. The mum was also new to her job. On her return to work she made a request to work four days instead of five, as compressed hours. Her request was accepted.

Was this unconscious bias at play? Was it considered more acceptable for her to work flexibly, because she was the mum? Was it just a different employer with different business needs? We will never know, but it's always left a question in their minds. If the dad had instead been the mum asking for a flexible work arrangement, would the employer have said no?

Historically, flexible work requests were fairly predictable and relatively infrequent. For example, a request from somebody in the team returning from parental leave, or with an elderly parent with an increasing need for care. These significant life events only happen a handful of times for most of us over an entire lifetime, which meant the flex requests weren't happening every day from everyone.

In that context, we didn't need to have a heavy process to make a decision when these one-off requests came up. As managers, we were able to deal with them easily and in an ad hoc way. A heavy team discussion for a flex request would have been the proverbial sledgehammer to crack a walnut. If a team member wanted to reduce their working hours by 20 per cent for six months, then a quick chat one-on-one with each team member would typically suffice to make sure the arrangement was going to be manageable for everyone.

Flex for all

Today, flexible work is for everyone. It's no longer the exception. So many people now have higher expectations about their autonomy over their hours, days and place of work. This creates a lot more movement and it's becoming increasingly complex to manage.

There are so many variables. People have different preferences from each other even though they might do the same job. Others within and outside the team have varying expectations of those in your team, and you can't keep up with what they all need and how that changes over time. A quick chat to check a one-off request simply doesn't cut it anymore.

I remember how I felt as a manager when someone came to me with a new flexible work request. I would start wondering about the fairness of saying yes, or no. I call that the equity conundrum. I would find myself asking questions like:

"If I say yes to this person, who am I effectively saying no to next time?"

"Is it fair to allocate flexible work requests simply on a first come first served basis?"

"If I say no will they just leave anyway, and I'll have a bigger problem to solve, recruiting and training a replacement?"

I would also have questions about the impact on delivery for the person asking for flexibility as well as the rest of the team who might need to pick up some additional work. I call this the **delivery doubt**.

"How can I test this idea with all the people that this team member connects with?"

"Will this create an unreasonable delivery expectation for others in the team?"

"Will I need to recruit a new person to maintain delivery standards?"

Shifting management of flex teams

When you're at the centre holding the control, the equity conundrum and delivery doubt often combine to constrain flexible work decisions in practice. We make small, incremental and conservative flexible work decisions as a way of reducing the risk we see from greater flexibility.

Participate in and facilitate

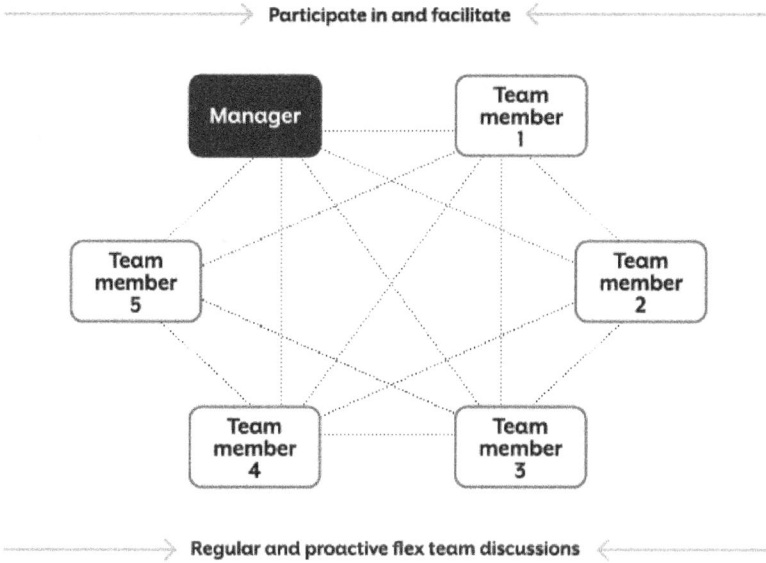

Regular and proactive flex team discussions

To get away from these issues, I see the core shift you make as the manager as going from a point of control in the centre, as shown above, to facilitating and participating from the side, as shown below.

Delivery doubt: Uncertainty about delivery assurance

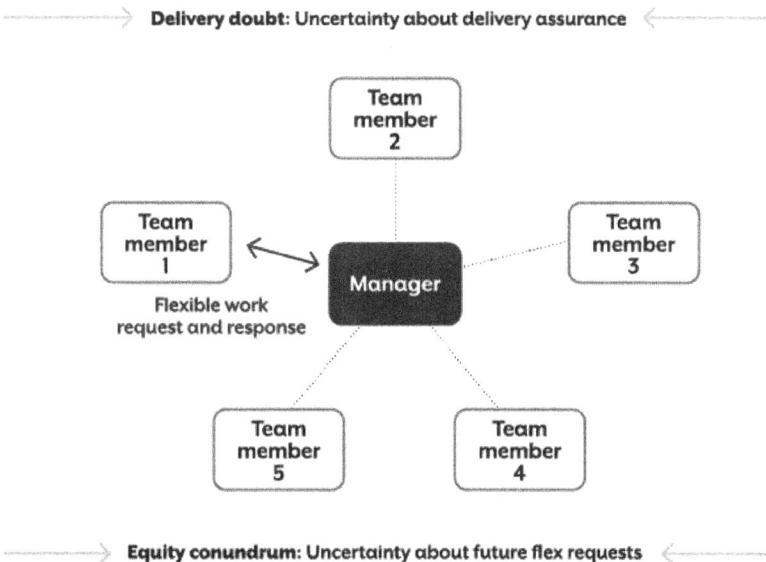

Flexible work
request and response

Equity conundrum: Uncertainty about future flex requests

Team-based decisions

From this position, away from the centre and alongside your team, you can facilitate and participate in regular, proactive and structured team-based conversations. In this role, you can open up the creativity of what flex can do for your whole team, including you. That's not to say you're no longer the decision maker – you are and should be. It's simply that the quality of input into your decision is so much richer and assuring when the team has had a high-quality conversation. The benefits of wellbeing and productivity follow when people are safe to explore a wider variety of options that might work best for them in and beyond their work life.

Case study

A former trade union organiser told me about a time when he was negotiating a more flexible roster on behalf of members. The managers and union could not agree on a roster pattern and they'd reached a deadlock. The employer was very clear about the delivery needs for the business and the union knew what their members wanted, and there was a big gap in the middle. They had reached an impasse.

The union side said, "What if we give members three weeks to design a roster they will sign up to that also meets your delivery parameters? Let's see what they come up with."

The employer side was sceptical but agreed to give it a try. After only five days, a new roster was proposed and subsequently agreed. It met the needs of the business and gave everyone a bit more of what they wanted to manage their life-demands outside of work. Both managers and the union were surprised to see what some individuals had agreed to. Those who were known for night shifts had opted for other arrangements. In many instances, people's lives had moved on but they hadn't spoken up about it and so were working around a shift pattern that no longer worked for them and their preferences. This gave them that opportunity to reset without having to single themselves out in the workplace.

The way most teams still operate, with the manager at the centre of all these moving parts, creates an impossibly complex burden. This worked fine in the old world, but it is no longer fit for purpose, nor is it fair or feasible for you, as the manager, to carry that burden on your own. You're not closest to the work to have the best view of what is possible and what isn't. The person best placed to test what's possible is the person themselves. But they need some tools to help them structure that in a way that gives you the assurance you need.

Chapter 6 outlines in detail the core flex-team tools that your team members can use to make sure they can give you the assurance you need that delivery is covered, while also giving them tools to make sure they're seeking flexible work options that fit with their personal preferences to give them a boost for their own wellbeing.

Chapter 7 provides the detail for you to prepare for and facilitate these team conversations. It's your roadmap to getting these conversations happening regularly and proactively.

Chapter summary

- Flex was reserved for the few until relatively recently.
- Flex is now something most people want and expect.
- Our approach to making flexible work decisions is outdated and no longer fit for purpose.
- As the manager, you can no longer get the most from flex by controlling from the centre with ad hoc, bilateral flexible work decisions.
- The best place for you to facilitate and participate is from the side.
- Having regular, proactive and structured team-based conversations will open up new flex possibilities for your team, and the benefits of productivity and wellbeing will follow.

-

"We'll wait until this thing goes away and we'll go back to normal." When you do that, you never prepare and you never develop the skills necessary to do this well."

Tsedal Neeley, *HBR*

Chapter 6

Flex tools

Although you've already seen a lot of the Flex-Team Toolkit, this chapter explores the critical, core tools that you and your team can reliably use in your regular, proactive team discussions.

In the last chapter we talked about the importance of a team discussion as critical input to the decisions you make about how to make flex work, and achieve the win-win described in Chapter 3.

To make sure people can get the outcome they're looking for, and stay in the high-trust, win-win quadrant, they need to know what to bring into the discussion. This builds credibility as part of the trust equation, which we touched on in Chapter 3. If people are credible about the ideas they bring into the discussion, everyone can invest in the process and trust that it will deliver more of what they are hoping for.

That's what this chapter is all about. There are tried and tested core tools here to help the people in your team uncover and explore what a win looks like for them and others around them. When they're clear about that, they can come into the team conversation with confidence that they can get creative with flexible work ideas that sit within the boundaries of what others need, as well as what they need themselves to be at their best.

With freedom comes responsibility

Before we get into the specific tools, it's worth spending some time emphasising how they need to be used. Using and applying these tools is the responsibility that each team member needs to take on, in exchange for the freedom that comes with greater levels of flexibility.

My favourite quote to highlight the established relationship between freedom and responsibility is from Eleanor Roosevelt:

"Freedom makes a huge requirement of every human being. With freedom comes responsibility."
Eleanor Roosevelt

Making it clear that it is the responsibility of each member of the team to take these tools, proactively use them, and bring the result back to the team conversation, is critical to the success of this approach to flexible work.

Without taking on this responsibility, it isn't a team approach anymore. Instead, it defaults back to the old, outdated model, with the manager at the centre, making the best decision they can, served only by limited information.

In my experience, team members understand this exchange between freedom and responsibility. They want to do the work required, if it means they get to access more flex options for themselves, now and in the future.

Valid flex options

These core tools fit into **two categories**:

1. **Delivery**

   Based on what is expected of you, right now, in your role.

2. **Wellbeing**

   What you gain when you're able to understand and work in ways that fit your situation and preferences.

The intersection of these two ideas is where the flex gold lies – a combination of what you need and what your job requires. This is the place to find the best flexible work options for you and your team members.

Let's take a look at the tools in these two categories: **Delivery** and **Wellbeing**
.

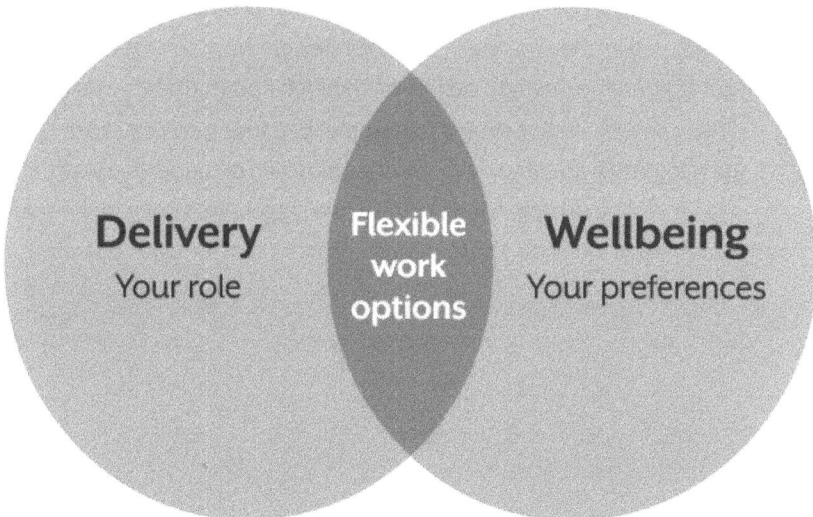

Delivery Your role — **Flexible work options** — **Wellbeing** Your preferences

Category 1
Delivery

You've probably been a manager long enough to know that a person's job description is the least useful document you can go to if you want to understand the work that they actually do every day. It's not that job descriptions don't have an important function – they do. They set the person's role within the context of the organisation's structure and pur- pose. It outlines at a high level what someone is responsible for and the kind of skills and experience they are likely to need to be successful.

This is great for recruitment. Beyond that, it's limited in its use.

The work people do every day is often a lot more fluid than our job descriptions can cover or keep up with. Things change, new priorities emerge, systems get updated and we all adapt accordingly. This cycle has become very familiar. Fluidity, ambiguity and adaptability have become corporate buzzwords for a reason!

With that in mind I saw that people need a timely way of making their job, as it currently stands, visible to themselves and others. Only by doing that can people assure themselves and others around them, especially you as their manager, that their flexible work arrangements are still going to enable them to deliver on their job commitments every day.

This can feel overwhelming for people, because they can't easily get all the things they are holding in their heads down on paper in a way that makes sense. I have broken it down into two stages. We start with people and then move into how those people connect to their everyday work.

Landscape of expectations

I start with people because, if a win-win is based on a scenario where high trust is nurtured, then it's clear that human relationships are at the heart of making flexible work a success.

Another myth perpetuated by our job descriptions and organisational structure is that you, as the manager, are the only person who has expectations of the people in your team. You'll know how ridiculous that idea is in reality. Yes, you are the person who sets the scope of someone's work for the upcoming period of time, but on a day-to-day basis, as the work gets delivered, success is so often dependent upon meeting the expectations of many, many other people besides you.

There are so many expectations flying around, inside and outside your workplace, that have no regard for our fictional systems or structures. That's where the idea for the landscape of expectations comes from. It's to keep up with that reality and make it visible.

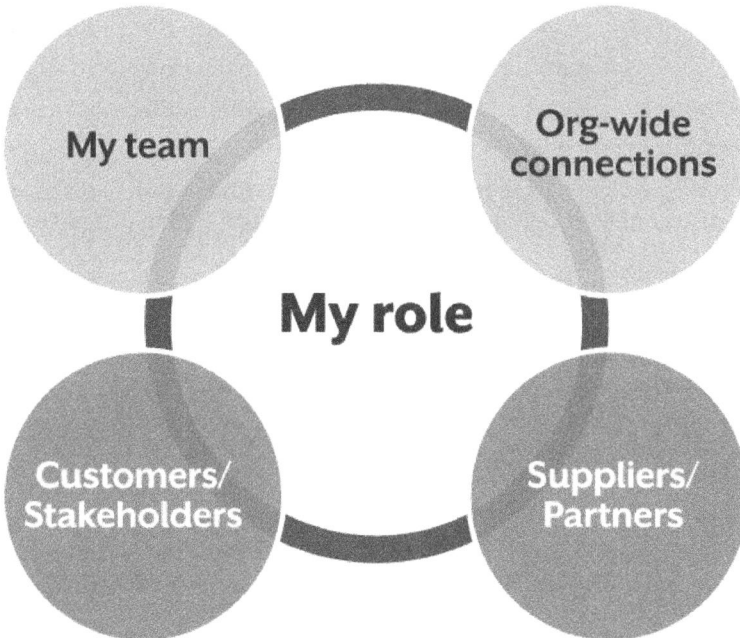

This landscape is designed to help the people in your team think about the people they work with most over a regular week or fortnight. The map is divided up with those inside the organisation at the top and those outside at the bottom.

The idea is that people regularly reflect on who they rely on and who relies on them to get work done. Taking those people into account before making flexible work decisions helps make sure the arrangements can be fully supported.

Using the downloadable template, they write the names of those relevant people across all parts of the landscape. Once the names are written down, the next stage is to reflect on how aligned they believe their expectations are with each person. They judge for themselves how well aligned they believe they are about how, when and where their work is done. They do this through an alignment score, with 10 being high and completely aligned, and one being low and no alignment at all. If the alignment score is high, this means there are well-established expectations in terms of when, where and how work gets done. It also means there is more likely to be a strong, high-trust working relationship.

If the alignment score is low, this means the working relationship is unclear and the expectations about when, where and how work gets done are relatively unexplored.

A low alignment score means a high risk of being perceived as 'entitled' by one of their colleagues. When that risk is high there is a danger of a backfire when making flexible work decisions.

Encouraging team members to prioritise conversations with people in their landscape who currently have a low alignment score is the best way forward. This will edge closer to higher alignment scores across the whole landscape for everyone in your team. The aim is for progress, not perfection. There will never be 100 per cent alignment between all people all of the time. But if there is a risk that it could create a delivery problem, it's a quick and easy way to work out what conversations need to happen to put that right.

Once they've done that they can move to the next tool, which explores the work they do every day.

Delivery assurance

The work we do in a typical week or fortnight can shift and change quite a lot over a year. If flexible work needs to ensure delivery of the work, the best place to start is to make the work visible and enable it to be updated as often as necessary. First, it needs to be visible to you, and then to others. This creates the assurance you and others are looking for that there won't be a new delivery gap to plug when you or someone in your team decides to change their hours, days or place of work.

Here is an example of the tried and tested tool I've developed to make this easy with descriptions of how to use it underneath.

What	How much	Who	How	When	Where
Core delivery area	Proportion of role	Connects with	Delivered via	Delivery time	Location
Helpdesk enquires	55%	Customers	Phone system	Scheduled	Office only
Project work	10%	IT team	Computer and email	Flexible	Office/home
Team and colleague interactions	20%	My team and	Face-to-face (10%)	Scheduled	Office only
		IT team	Email (10%)	Flexible	Office/home
Supplier management	10%	Phone system provider	Email	Flexible	Office/home
Training programme	5%	External IT network	Face-to-face	Scheduled	Off-site

- 65% of the role has fixed, scheduled work that is office-based only.
- 30% of the role is flexible with time, days and place.
- Through agreed scheduling it's possible to have working from home arrangments 1-day per week.
- Flexible hours also possible one day per week.
- Use team-based proactive discussions to explore how this could work.

What: core delivery area

The first column is a list of the core chunks of work that you're responsible for and what you spend your time doing in a typical week or fortnight at the moment. It's important to remember to include professional development here too. As we highlighted in Chapter 4, one of the key challenges emerging with flex is the plight of the 'lonely learner'. By making the learning visible in this way it is much more likely to be factored in when making flexible work decisions.

How much: proportion of role

This is where you give an approximate time allocation to each chunk of the role, based on how the work is being delivered at the moment. In addition to being clear about how the work is playing out from a time perspective, it can also be a useful calibration exercise. People feeling overwhelmed with delivery expectations often find they've already got to 100 per cent of their time before they've finished getting through the list of delivery areas. This is their cue to come and talk about resetting their priorities. As we explored in Chapter 4, flex can't solve the problem of too much work and over-commitment. This tool helps to highlight where this delivery pressure is coming from and gives you an opportunity to recalibrate those expectations for people in this situation.

Who: connects with

This is where you put the names from the 'Landscape of Expectations' tool next to the relevant piece of the delivery puzzle. The point here is to make sure that the alignment conversations that people have with others in their landscape are focused and valuable. What we want to avoid is everybody talking to everyone about the full extent of their role. This would become exhausting and put people off using the toolkit altogether. Make sure you encourage people in their alignment conversations to only focus on the relevant pieces of delivery so they make good use of each other's time.

How: delivered via

This is for you to clarify the system or method used to deliver the various areas of delivery. Some areas might be a mix, for example, team interactions might be split between face-to-face and online, which is worth noting because it has an implication for where work can be delivered from.

When: delivery time

Here you consider the extent of the time-autonomy you have over each area of delivery. There is often a combination of 'flexible' or 'fixed' delivery commitments when it comes to the timing of the work you do. This is the place to note which things are scheduled or fixed and which are more flexible, as long as they are delivered by an agreed time. The fixed, scheduled work needs to be given assurance and acts as a constraint to the hours or days that you work. The flexible areas of work provide the opportunity to be more open and creative about when the work is delivered.

Where: location

Depending on the work you do, there can be only one or multiple location options. When this is visible it can be verified or challenged by other relevant people. Given that the biggest challenge people are experiencing with flex is feeling disconnected from their colleagues, as we saw in Chapter 3, location is an important factor to explore.

Delivery boundaries

The discussions that follow the completion of these delivery tools is an important part of the process. This is where the clear delivery boundaries are clarified and mutually understood by all the relevant people. Assumptions are tested and new boundaries are often drawn, creating new opportunities. Coming into this with a fixed mindset is the main risk to manage for people in your team and others within their 'landscape'. They may need some support from you, especially when this toolkit is new and unfamiliar. Over time, as these conversations become part of an established way of doing things, that need for your support will naturally fall away.

Category 2
Wellbeing

As I shared in the introduction, wellbeing economics has heavily influenced the way I think about how to get the best from flex.

In 1979, Amartya Sen, economist, philosopher and Nobel Laureate, developed the capability approach to wellbeing. Sen is considered the founding father of wellbeing economics.

The essence of the capability approach to wellbeing is freedom to choose. The freedom for people to 'be' and 'do' the things that they value and have reason to value. This true access to choice is central in Sen's work.

If wellbeing benefits are what you want to achieve for you and your team, then it's important for people to have valid choices available to them. Once delivery is assured, those choices become a safe place to explore for you and others in your team.

Tools, not rules

When people are given the freedom to choose, this is often when managers feel most vulnerable. It is stepping into the unknown, and it can feel like the control, and the comfortable ways of working we have all been accustomed to, start to fall away. This uncertainty trigger might give you the impulse to assert some rules, such as:

- you can only work from home a maximum of two days per week
- compressed hours are off the table
- job sharing is too complicated for us to manage
- part-time won't work for this team.

If you notice yourself coming up with these blanket rules, just pause for a moment. It is these rules that so often cut off valid options for a minority of people. If some people aren't given the opportunity to access the wellbeing benefits that others can, while still delivering on their role, flexible work will remain fragile and will never be fully trusted in your team.

When you notice yourself reaching for rules, instead rely on the tools. If something new is being explored by the team, try it out for an agreed period of time. The team will then come back again to review how it went, so you're not locking in something before it's been properly tested.

If wellbeing is at its best when we can each be and do what we value, then we each need to know what that is. Knowing what you want can often be the hardest thing to pinpoint. So rather than leave it open, there are some tools, grounded in research, to help you and your team work out what your personal preferences are and how they might differ from each other.

The two core **flex-team tools** help people to explore:

1.   Managing boundaries
   Healthy boundaries between work and home

2.   Remote work hack
   Being at your best when working remotely.

Flex-team tool 1: **Managing boundaries**

As we explored in Chapter 4, one of the challenges at the moment is unhealthy boundaries between work life and home life. It's true that this has been exacerbated by the pandemic, when so many people were suddenly working from home with no other choice available. When work and home were enforced into the same physical space, the boundaries became very difficult to manage. However, this isn't a new problem and pre-dates the pandemic by decades.

Technology that emerged in the 1980s began to blur the boundaries between work life and home life for the first time since the industrial revolution. This led to the development of boundary theory by academics1 who wanted to understand how people managed the boundaries between work and home. This led to a continuum, with two key preferences at either end: **segmenters** and **integrators**.

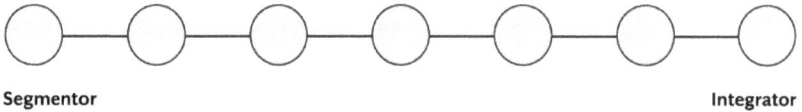

Segmentor   Integrator

Preferences

- **Segmenters** are people with a preference for behavioural and/or physical boundaries between work and home. Segmenters are less stressed when they have these clear boundaries in place.
- **Integrators** have a preference to permeate or be flexible with the boundaries between work and home. They are less stressed when they are able to do that.

One example I often use to describe how these preferences might show up at work is with the idea of a person given the option of having a work mobile phone.

A segmenter is more likely to want to have a work phone and a personal phone. Keeping these two devices separate means they will be less stressed. While in work mode they will happily keep their work phone with them and be responsive to it, as it beeps away. However, when they switch into home mode, they will turn the phone off, or put it away. This helps them manage their boundaries and their stress levels, getting a good lift to their wellbeing.

An integrator will most likely find the idea of two phones quite stressful. They would get annoyed with switching between two devices throughout the day and would much rather have everything in one digital place.

Our preferences can shift, depending on what else we have going on in our lives. A 2020 study carried out by Yasin Rofcanin at the University of Bath, Professor of Human Resource Management and Organisational Psychology at University of Bath, looked at how women, who carry a disproportionate share of caring responsibilities, have a preference for segmentation. What this shows is that the more 'life' you have going on, the more likely it is you'll need to segment home from work. This rule doesn't apply to everyone, but it shows that our preference might well change over time.

Most of us aren't pure segmenters or integrators. Most of us are somewhere in the middle. Knowing your personal preference is an important part of managing your boundaries so that you can lift your wellbeing through flexibility rather than risk moving into the burnout quadrant, as we explored in Chapter 3.

Reality

When you have worked out your preference, the next step is to test that against reality. If your reality and ideal preference line up, that is good news. If there's a gap then you're managing your boundaries outside your preference, and that is likely to cause you stress and reduce your sense of wellbeing.

When there's a gap between preference and reality, there's an invitation to think about what you can try, or what you can experiment with, that will narrow the gap.

When you're talking to your team members about this, encourage them to try one thing at a time and notice what works or what doesn't. When people are working outside their preference they are likely to already feel stressed. Heaping new work on that person to change their boundaries overnight, while well intended, could do more harm than good in the short term. Instead, focus their attention on testing and learning through short-lived experiments designed to find out what works best for them.

Team cohesion

When each person shares their insights with their team there are often 'aha' moments for everyone. When people understand their own and each other's boundaries they are much more likely to show empathy and support to help each person work as close as possible to their preference. This is another brick to build on the high-trust culture that flex benefits thrive in. It takes us into considering others rather than self-orientation. Self-orientation undermines trust, as we touched on in Chapter 3 with the trust equation.

Case study

A manager using this tool for the first time told me that everyone in her team reported that their preference and reality were completely aligned, and they felt that their work and home boundaries were being managed really well.

Her own experience was the complete opposite. Her preference was for more segmentation than she was experiencing in reality.

Sharing this 'aha' moment with her team meant that, for the first time, she was participating in, not just facilitating, getting the best from flex. The others in the team started asking how they could help and exploring what she needed from them to narrow the gap. They agreed that she would no longer answer emails after 7pm and would put her phone in a drawer at weekends. Immediately this made a difference to her stress levels and also reinforced the importance of managing boundaries for everyone in the team, including the manager.

Flex-team tool 2: **Remote work**

As you will have grasped by now, flexible work is about having choices regarding the hours, days and/or place of work. For some of us, place isn't a very useful variable. That might be because the work we do doesn't lend itself to working from home. We might be client facing, or constrained by security requirements. Alternatively we might have work that is easily delivered from home, but our preference is to segment work and home with the physical boundary making permanent use of the office.

Having said that, remote work is still a hot topic. There is an expectation that remote and hybrid work will form a much bigger part of our future than it did in our pre-pandemic past. At the time of writing, approximately 30 per cent of paid work is being done from home and appears to be stabilising at this level.[2]

If remote work is going to feature a lot more, there are some useful insights to help us avoid the known pitfalls and get the best out of it.

There is a lot of research and interest in this topic. As I've trawled my way through, I've landed on three key areas of remote work that can get in the way of us being at our best. I summarise them as:

- **Connect:** staying connected to our colleagues
- **Work:** the type of work we tend to focus on
- **Well:** putting good boundaries in place to be at our best.

Connect

There's a famous TED Ex talk by Nick Bloom, from 2017, in which he out-lines the benefits of remote work – higher levels of productivity, as well as higher levels of retention, with people staying longer in their job. The biggest downside from remote work was that people felt isolated.

My own research, found that the biggest challenge by far was that people felt disconnected from their colleagues.

The more you can do to focus people on connecting and collabo-rating with each other, the better. It might be formal collaboration that people commit to by attending meetings with their colleagues, contrib-uting and being fully present throughout. Or it might be informal connec-tions to establish and maintain strong, healthy working relationships.

Work

When working from home, people tend to focus on task-based, short-term productivity activities, as described in Chapter 3.

To avoid falling into that trap, it's important to commit time to imag-inative, creative work. This leads to ideas that ultimately create new and different ways for our organisations to deliver value. It's the driver of long-term productivity that we also explored in Chapter 3.

Well

Finally, the known problem of poor boundaries between work and home was covered in the boundary tool. It's here to help people connect these ideas specifically to when they are working remotely and remember that boundaries are critical to being at their best.

Remote work hack

The way to use this tool is to ask people to think about their answers to two questions:

- What is working well for you, keeping you on the solution side at the moment when you're working from home?
- Where are your potential problem areas at the moment that you'd like some help to solve?

Ask them to write down their answers to these questions. In the team, invite everyone to share their responses. When everyone has shared, let the conversation and connections flow until everyone has at least one new idea to take away and try that will upgrade their remote work experience.

Repeat this as often as you need to and keep the fresh ideas flowing!

Problem		Solution
Isolation	Connect	Collaboration
Repetition	Work	Imagination
Exhaustion	Well	Animation

Chapter summary

- It is the responsibility of every person in the team to use the core flex-team tools ahead of the flex-team discussion.
- These core tools give team members safe boundaries within which to explore flexible work options.
- Flexible work options are the overlap between '**delivery**' and '**wellbeing**'.

- '**Delivery**' involves:

  » aligning expectations between all the relevant people
  » clarifying what work needs delivering
  » exploring the flexibility available within the constraints of the work to be done.

- '**Wellbeing**' involves:

  » understanding personal preferences to manage boundaries between work and home
  » avoiding the known pitfalls of working from home.

Chapter 6 notes

1 www.researchgate.net/profile/Russell-Matthews-2/publication/5893241_Work_and_
   Personal_Life_ Boundary_Management_Boundary_Strength_WorkPersonal_Life_Balance_
   and_the_Segmentation-Integr ation_Continuum/links/57bda03108ae37ee394baa9c/
   Work-and-Personal-Life-Boundary-Management-Bo undary-Strength-Work-Personal-Life-
   Balance-and-the-Segmentation-Integration-Continuum.pdf
2 https://wfhresearch.com/wp-content/uploads/2022/01/Barrero-AEA-NABE-Jan22.pdf

"Keep asking your employees for their views... This can elicit revelatory conversations."
Andrew Barnes, *4 Day Week*

Chapter 7
Flex manager guide

Flex-team cycle

Now you have the core tools you need, it's a case of getting into the practical application of them for you and your team.

Below is a suggested workflow to help you prepare for and facilitate regular, proactive flex-team discussions.

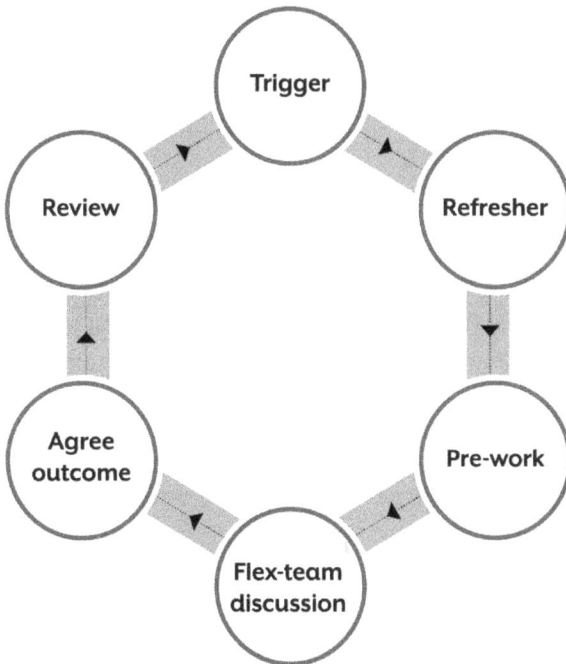

Stage 1
Trigger

A flex-team discussion should ideally take place every six months, depending on the nature of your work. If there is variation in your team's work with seasonality or other cycles, it's worth triggering a flex-team discussion in line with that natural rhythm of work.

Other events that might act as triggers include:

- a new starter joining the team
- someone changing roles within the team
- someone returning from a period of extended leave
- new or different work coming into the team
- a new system that changes how work is delivered.

Stage 2
Refresher

This is the time for you to remind people of the tools and how to use them. When this is new to the team it will take more support from you to help them become familiar with the tools. As this becomes part of your regular team practice it will be a much easier part of the process. New starters will always need a bit more support if they haven't used these tools before.

Stage 3
Pre-work

Give each team member two weeks to complete their pre-work, using the tools in Chapter 6.

Stage 4

Flex-team discussion

The main event! This is when everyone in the team brings their pre-work and is ready to share the flexible work arrangements they'd like to explore.

As you facilitate and participate in this discussion you might find this suggested agenda a useful place to begin

Flex-team discussion agenda

This is a simple option to get you and your team started with a flex-team discussion.

Flex perceptions

1. What score out of 10 would you give our team for successful flex?
2. Share and reflect on scores.

Move flex forward

1. **What:** Each person shares their preferred flexible work options from their pre-work.
2. **How:** Discuss how tools, tech and teamwork commitments can be used to enable more flex possibilities.
3. Agree outcomes and measures to track progress.
4. Decide on a review date.

What	How
• Hours	• Technology
• Days	• Tools
• Place	• Teamwork

The beginning of the discussion focuses on reviewing how flex has been going since the last flex-team discussion. An easy way into this is to ask everyone to give flex a score out of 10 before the conversation begins. Ask each person to reflect on why they gave that score.

Follow up questions can be helpful if there isn't much discussion forthcoming, such as:

- *What is the biggest challenge to flex at the moment?*
- *What is the best thing you've learnt about making flex successful recently?*

Then you shift into the '**Move flex forward**' part of the agenda.

This is where you hear from each person about what they would like to explore and why. You have options here to ask people to share their insights from both the 'Delivery' and 'Wellbeing' tools. Giving the team the space to share how they reached their decisions about how they want to move flex forward will build more empathy and strengthen the connections and working relationships in the team. If your flex-team discussion has been triggered by a new starter arriving in the team, then it is worth taking the time to share the insights from the full set of tools. It is a powerful part of the induction process for newbies, accelerating their ability to do their work and have a sense of belonging with their new colleagues.

What and how of flex

The '**what**' will be the hours, days and place of work that people want to adopt or try out. The '**how**' is more about the enablers of flex. These often come up as ideas that remove existing barriers or challenges with flex.

When thinking about how to enable more options for you and your team, the enablers, or how work gets done, are an important part of the puzzle. More enablers means more flex options, as a general rule.

In the work I do I've learnt to categorise the enablers into three distinct groups: **technology**, **tools** and **teamwork**.

Top tip

It's often beyond your immediate control to determine which technology and tools you have access to or invest in as an organisation. Those decisions most often sit with the senior leaders responsible for property, facilities and technology. Having your flex-team discussions is an ideal place to begin to build a case. If your team reaches the same insights and has identified an enabler that matches that of other teams, you'll be well placed to put an investment case forward for key changes that will keep moving flex forward, giving access to more benefits. Bringing together your heads of technology, property and facilities, finance and human resources all under the banner of 'Employee Experience' is a useful frame to the conversation.

Technology

There are two different purposes behind technology enablers to support greater flexibility. One is to connect people virtually in real time, or synchronously, when they are working from disparate locations. This saw the explosion of tech platforms such as Zoom and MS Teams to host meetings and collaborate. There is another driver which is to support asynchronous team work. This is when work gets done collaboratively but people contribute at different times. There is a lot more opportunity for us to experiment with asynchronous work if we want to get even more creative with flex. If we are overly reliant on people working together at the same time, we severely limit flex options.

One example I use is voice notes on the WhatsApp platform. If I need to have a conversation with someone but our schedules are unlikely to match up in a timely way, I record a voice message, with my thoughts, questions, reflections, etc. When the other person (or people) in that group are available, they can listen and respond with their contribution. The process continues for as many messages as needed. I use this more and more. It's got all the nuance of voice, which I find richer than email, but we don't have to wait to be available at the same time to progress our work.

Tools

People need new and different tools, or physical equipment, to fit with greater flexibility. They might need some computer and desk equipment at home as well as in the office. More and more office spaces are operating with flexible desk spaces.

With so many people working different hours and days, as well as many more commonly working from home, office spaces can feel lonely and empty as well as unnecessarily expensive due to their under-utilisation. This is in tension with people's sense of belonging when they do come into the office. People like to feel 'at home' with their designated space.

Acknowledging that loss and providing easy-to-set-up flexible desk spaces for quiet, concentrated work and new collaboration spaces to encourage people to make the most of face-to-face contact with each other is a good way forward. What are some of the tools and equipment you might commit to as enablers in your workplace?

Teamwork

This concerns the commitments the team members make to each other that will enable a greater chance of success with flexible work options. For example, to make sure the team stays connected beyond immediate tasks and still has high-quality working relationships, members might decide to have a shared lunch once a month, or commit to a 30-minute team chat every other day where the only rule is that no-one is allowed to talk about work. Or the team might agree that everyone will prioritise group work on the one day everyone comes into the office to make the most of the fact everyone is in the same physical space on that day.

The 'what' and 'how' of flex support each other. As you explore new types of flex, new enablers emerge and as new enablers become available, you'll be able to explore new and different types of flex options. This can be usefully framed as getting the best decisions for 'me' and 'we'.

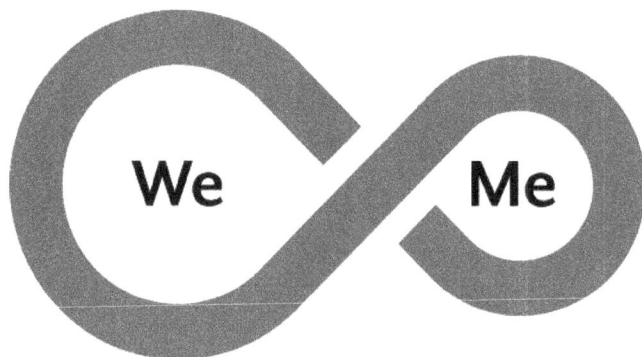

For each of us to be at our individual best, we also need to commit to some collective choices. These will inevitably create tension between 'me' and 'we' at times. For the whole team to thrive it's important to get the balance right. If your team needs to explore this balance further, check out the 'Me & We' template in the flex-team toolkit.

Stage 5
Agree outcome

Ultimately, the decisions about flex are yours to make. You're the manager with the accountability to deliver the work required of you and your team. However, as we explored in Chapter 5, going it alone with ad hoc information and bilateral conversation is severely limiting and constrains what's possible when it comes to flex benefits.

The main benefit of the flex-team discussion is to give you the richest possible input to those decisions. In most instances, as you facilitate and participate in the discussion, the outcomes and their rationale are clear to everyone. It is important to follow up the discussion with recorded outcomes and share them in writing across everyone in the team. This avoids any misinterpretations of the agreed outcomes and keeps everyone feeling safe to try out whatever was agreed.

If it has been agreed that a new and bold idea will be tried and tested, there might be a time-bound trial. Any trial will ideally have clear and agreed measures of success. Keep these as simple as possible and use the tools to guide you. For example, if people in the team's landscape of expectations agree that the trial is working from their perspective, you might use that as your measure.

You can also use the regular flex perception measure outlined in the beginning of the Flex-Team Discussion Agenda, as well as in Chapter 2. This is the question that asks each team member to share their score out of 10 that reflects how well flex is going. Tracking how that score moves over time is often the most powerful and simplest way to discover what is working well and what is in need of an upgrade.

In the absence of pre-agreed measures of success, it can get complicated when the trial is up for review. If everyone has their own idea of success it can be impossible to agree whether or not to adopt the tested idea into regular practice.

Stage 6
Review

Review any trials in line with what was agreed in your flex-team discussion. If it was a success it's likely the team will keep the new practice. If it was not, it might lead the team to try out something else instead and lead into the next round of your flex-team cycle.

Exceptions

The proactive flex-team discussion is a powerful input into decisions you make. People in your team will still request flexible work at any time and they often won't wait for a scheduled team discussion to make their request.

If and when that happens it's a good idea to have a team conversation to test what is possible and how other potential moving parts across the team can free up options for more flex. People might be holding unknown preferences, but haven't yet felt them strongly enough to test with you and their colleagues.

There are situations when the flexible work request is too sensitive to trigger an open flex-team discussion. As the manager, you have the discretion to make bilateral flexible work agreements with anyone in your team. This is best held as the exception and if the person in the team is comfortable sharing a little of their context with their team, that often helps to accommodate their flexible work request without any misunderstandings that can create resentment in the team.

For example, if someone has a new health condition they need to manage, sharing that headline might generate enough empathy from others in the team to help the colleague get what they need without any need for full disclosure of the nature of that condition. Other examples can include a relationship break-up or a bereavement that means the person will be at their best with a different work arrangement in the short to medium term.

Chapter summary

- Flex-team discussions ideally happen every six months.
- They can also be triggered by other events, such as a new starter joining the team.
- People might need your support to refresh themselves on how to use the flex-team tools.
- Your role in the flex-team discussion is to facilitate and participate.
- The discussion will explore both the 'what' and 'how' of flex.
- The 'what' of flex explores the hours, days and place of work.
- The 'how', or enablers, of flex fall into three categories:

  » technology
  » tools
  » teamwork.

- The agreed outcome of the flex-team discussion needs to be followed up in writing.
- If a time-bound trial of a new form of flex has been agreed, also agree the measures of success in advance.
- Remember to complete the review of any trials in line with what was agreed.
- There are exceptions to the flex-team discussion cycle, which you can use your discretion to manage.

"Learning is an active process.
We learn by doing… Only
knowledge that is used sticks
in your mind."
Dale Carnegie

Flexpert in training

Conclusion

It's not just you! Everyone finds managing a flexible team challenging in some way and at some time. Becoming a flexpert takes time and practice, just like anything else. We've never before needed to give it so much of our time and attention. You're ahead of the game now, though. You've got the tools, templates and resources you need to build up your flexpertise.

People in the human resources team often don't have the time and resources to go deep on solving this with a comprehensive set of tools and resources. That is why I did this work, because I wanted to go deep and solve it at scale.

These tools are tried and tested as a solid starting point for you and your team. Feel free to adapt them as you learn what works best. Let me know how you get on; you can find me easily on LinkedIn or via my website at **www.gillianbrookes.co.nz.**

I've only built these tools through researching and synthesising my ideas with those of others, mixed in with a good measure of endless testing with real-life people, just like you.

Go well and good luck as you fuel up your team's ability to work more flexibly with more of the benefits of productivity and wellbeing. You'll be a flexpert in no time!

Appendix

Flex-team toolkit

Index of downloads

To download these 20 flex resources and templates go to:
www.flexteamtoolkit.com

Tool **Workforce distribution cake** (page 19)

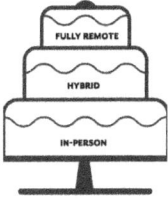

Purpose Identify which part of the workforce your team fits into: in-person; hybrid; fully remote.

How to use it The workforce is dividing into three layers. Use the cake to determine which layer or layers of the cake your team or teams are part of.

Core? No

Tool **Flex menu** (page 22)

Flex menu

Flexi-hours
Working daily or weekly hours in a flexible way, such as flexing start and finish times, or taking a longer lunch break. May include core hours in the middle of the day.

Part-time
Regularly working a fixed portion and fewer hours than the standard full-time working week.

Compressed hours

Purpose Defines different types of flex that you and your team can explore.

How to use it In your flex-team discussions use this menu to explore which types of flex you could try and which you're not ready for yet.

Core? Yes

Tool **Flex maturity** (page 31)

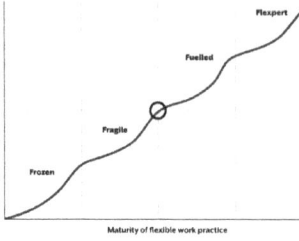

Purpose Identify which stage of flex maturity you are at in your organisation or team.

How to use it Using the descriptors of each stage of maturity, identify which stage your team and organisation are at.

Use the reflection questions in the template to discuss the implications and possible actions for you and your team.

Core? No

Tool **Fuelling flex** (page 37)

Purpose Explore three key ingredients to fuel flex in your team and organisation.

How to use it Identify what might be causing flex to fail and discover what needs to happen to fuel flex in your team or organisation.

Core? No

Tool **Measuring flex – Strategy** (page 41)

Tool **Measuring flex – Reality** (page 41)

Tool **Measuring flex – Perception** (page 42)

Purpose Identify the measures required to track flex and its impact in your team or organisation.

How to use it

Use the templates to:

1. Measure the strategic intent for flex in your team
2. Measure how flex is perceived by people in your team
3. Measure the uptake of flex in your team.

Core? No

Tool **Flex leadership** (page 44)

Purpose Identify your own flex leadership style including its strengths and common pitfalls to watch out for.

How to use it   Use the descriptors and reflection exercise to identify your dominant flex leadership style and gain insight about the benefits and common pitfalls you're likely to experience.

Core? No

Tool **Flex scenario map** (page 60)

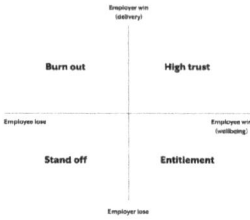

Purpose Describe and identify which flex scenarios are playing out in your team at the moment.

Core? Yes

Tool **Hybrid productivity** (page 70)

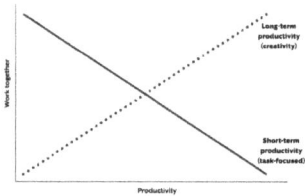

Purpose Consider how flex can support both short-term and long-term productivity across the team.

How to use it Find your optimal productivity through getting the best hybrid work mix of in-person versus remote work.

Core? No

Tool **Lonely learners** (page 79)

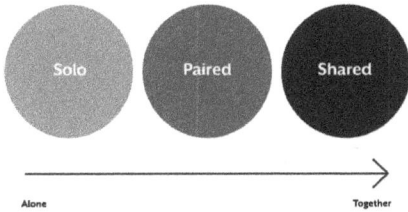

Solo   Paired   Shared

Alone   Together

Purpose Identify how to maintain focus on induction and professional development in a flexible team.

How to use it Consider the activities you need to support your development goals across this simple three-part framework.

Core? No

Tool **Flex teams** (page 93)

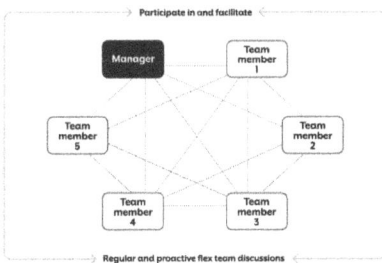

Participate in and facilitate

Manager   Team member 1

Team member 5   Team member 2

Team member 4   Team member 3

Regular and proactive flex team discussions

Purpose Illustrate the team dynamics for a successful flex-team discussion.

How to use it Describe and discuss with your team why a regular and proactive flex-team discussion is better for everyone.

Core? Yes

Tool **Valid flex options** (page 101)

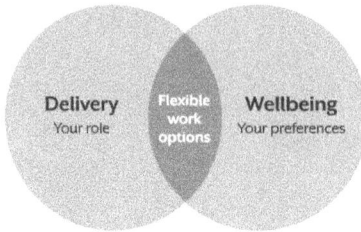

Purpose Summarise your valid flex options to share in your
Flex Team discussion.

How to use it Do the work to explore your own wellbeing
and delivery first. Then use those insights to define the valid flex
options you want to explore in your Flex Team discussion.

Core? Yes

Tool **Landscape of expectations** (page 103)

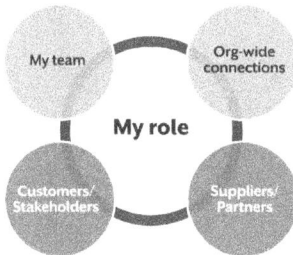

Purpose Explore who has expectations of you and how well
aligned you are with each other's expectations about how, when
and where work is delivered.

How to use it Identify the strength of the alignment between you
and others. Use this alongside the 'Delivery Assurance' template
to guide your discussions and calibrate expectations between you
and other important people in your delivery landscape.

Core? Yes

Tool **Delivery assurance** (page 105)

What	How much	Who	How	When	Where
Core delivery area	Proportion of role	Connects with	Delivered via	Delivery time	Location
Helpdesk enquires	55%	Customers	Phone system	Scheduled	Office only
Project work	10%	IT team	Computer and	Flexible	Office/home

Purpose Discover clear boundaries within which to play with your flex options. Consider the work you do every day before you decide which flex options are on or off the menu for you.

How to use it Identify the work and professional development you're committed to before you decide which flex options you would like to explore further.

Core? Yes

Tool **Managing boundaries** (page 110)

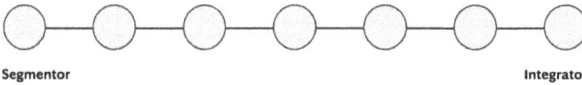

Segmentor   Integrator

Purpose Understand your preference around boundary management and whether or not you are working within or outside your preference.

How to use it Identify your preference and reality when it comes to boundary management. If there is a gap, try experimenting with ways to shift your reality closer towards your preference.

Core? Yes

Tool **Remote work hack** (page 116)

Problem		Solution
Isolation	Connect	Collaboration
Repetition	Work	Imagination
Exhaustion	Well	Animation

Purpose Be at your best when working remotely by avoiding the common pitfalls.

How to use it 'Hack' this with your team to avoid the common pit-falls and share the things that keep you at your best.

Core? Yes

Tool **Flex-team cycle** (page 119)

Trigger · Refresher · Pre-work · Flex-team discussion · Agree outcome · Review

Purpose Keep the team on track with regular and proactive flex-team discussions, making time and space for prep and review.

How to use it Following this flex-team cycle will ensure you're having regular and proactive flex-team discussions supported by good preparation and solid reviews.

Core? Yes

Tool **Flex-team discussion agenda** (page 121)

What	How
Hours	Technology
Days	Tools
Place	Teamwork

Purpose Explore both 'what' flex arrangements people would prefer as well as 'how' those arrangements can be enabled (or disabled).

How to use it In the flex-team discussion ask everyone to share their preferred flex arrangements (based on their pre-work) and explore what tech, tools and teamwork commitments you'll need to make it work.

Core? Yes

Tool **Teamwork** (page 126)

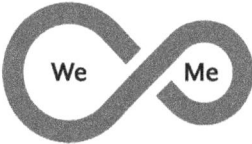

Purpose Operate flex in your team as a healthy ecosystem where individual and collective needs are considered and explored.

How to use it Explore the pain and gain of flex for 'me' and 'we'. Each individual completes the template ahead of the flex-team discussion. Then you can tease out tensions to ensure there is a healthy balance with flex supporting the whole team as well as each individual.

Core? Yes

Acknowledgements

Given this is the first time I've written a book, I have so many people to thank. I've had so much encouragement, support, welcome advice and expertise around me to make this possible. I already know that I will fail miserably to properly and sufficiently acknowledge everyone who played a role in getting Flexperts out into the world, but here goes.

First, I want to thank my editor, Sue Copsey. You've warmly encouraged me throughout the project and helped me banish any crippling sense of imposter syndrome. I have deeply valued your skill, craft, experience and wisdom to bring these words to life. Also, thanks for your excellent proofreading and feedback, Helen Greatrex.

Next, a big thank you to Greg Simpson, who has turned the design of the book and its graphics into something that looks like a grown up was in charge. Thank you so much. I just don't have that design brain and I am always in awe of those like you who do.

So many of my friends and family have encouraged, nudged and offered such valuable suggestions. Digby Scott, you always just get it and want me to be my best, which makes me believe a bit more that I can. Jenny Brown, for being my friend who reads more books than anyone else I know. Your practical suggestions have made the reading experience much more engaging for the reader. Anna Hughes and Jacqui Van Der Kaay, for helping me understand so much more about the written word and backing me to keep putting my words out there. Karaitiana Wilson, thank you for never failing to ask me how the book was progressing, giving me the accountability nudge I so often needed. Encouragement and accountability credit also go to Renee Jaine and Lisa Allen.

I want to thank the three people who volunteered to read the first draft of the book: Rebecca Foley, Jamie Shackleton and Katie Hair. Each of you gave so much thought and consideration to your feedback, which really helped me structure the book with my audience in mind.

So many people have inspired and influenced my thinking, making *Flexperts* possible; clients, big thinkers and those who share a passion for reshaping the future of work.

I want to thank all my clients for working with me over the last few years. Without you the content in this book simply wouldn't exist. I've learnt so much from testing and tweaking my ideas and tools alongside you.

The big thinkers who inspire me include Kate Raworth, for your incredible work on rethinking the economy. Also in that list I include Joseph Stiglitz, Katrine Marcal, Amartya Sen and Katherine Trebeck.

Those who inspire me every day with their influence on reshaping the future of work include Candice Harris, Jarrod Haar, Nick Bloom, Paula O'Kane, Alex Soojun-Kim Pang, Andrew Barnes and Charlotte Lockhart, Annie Auerbach, Gemma Dale, Belinda Morgan and Ellen Joan Nelson. You help me remember that I'm not going this alone and that other people are ready and willing to make bigger changes happen.

Last, but not least, my heart-level inspiration and acknowledgements. Mum, you have taught me to balance competing life demands, like the master you are. You showed me from a young age what it meant to be a working mum and you made time and space for me, no matter what else you had going on, in good times and bad. Emily and Lucy, you've taught me to be the mum that I am and inspire me every day to want bigger, bolder changes for the world. I'll do the little bit I can in the hope you and your generation inherit something better, just as my mum and her generation did for me and mine.

About the author

Gillian Brookes is a flexible work specialist and has run her consultancy practice since mid-2019. Prior to that Gillian had a successful career as a leader in human resources in both the UK and New Zealand, working across private, public, and not-for-profit sectors in a variety of industries.

Originally from the UK, Gillian lives in Wellington, New Zealand, and has two daughters, Emily and Lucy. She holds a BSc (hons) International Business Economics from Lancaster University and a Post-Graduate Diploma in Human Resource Management from Kingston University.

Flexperts is her first book. Other writing from Gillian has been published in New Zealand's *Sunday Star Times* and in her regular blog www.gillianbrookes.co.nz/blog.

www.ingramcontent.com/pod-product-compliance
Lightning Source LLC
Chambersburg PA
CBHW071557200326
41519CB00021BB/6790